ENTRUSTED

Stewardship for Responsible Wealth Creation

ONG BOON HWEE · MARK GOYDER

To Tony

without whose leadership
this wouldn't have happened.

Mark

18 July 2020.

 World Scientific

 STEWARDSHIP ASIA

Published by

World Scientific Publishing Co. Pte. Ltd.
5 Toh Tuck Link, Singapore 596224
USA office: 27 Warren Street, Suite 401-402, Hackensack, NJ 07601
UK office: 57 Shelton Street, Covent Garden, London WC2H 9HE

and

Stewardship Asia Centre CLG Limited
28 Orchard Road
Temasek Shophouse
Singapore 238832

Stewardship Asia Centre (SAC) is a thought leadership centre promoting effective stewardship and governance across Asia. Positioned to inspire and catalyse change, SAC builds capabilities and platforms that enable organisations to foster enduring success and responsible wealth creation for the long-term, and to benefit the wider community and future generations. SAC is a non-profit organisation established under the Temasek Trust. Visit www.stewardshipasia.com.sg for more details.

ENTRUSTED
Stewardship for Responsible Wealth Creation

ISBN 978-981-120-755-6
ISBN 978-981-120-756-3 (pbk)

Cover Design: Bamboo, in Asian cultures, is a symbol of vitality, resilience and wealth. Firmly rooted, bamboo bends under pressure but does not break. Bamboo takes time to grow sturdy roots before its shoots surface. After which, they develop rapidly. Bamboo thrives in tough and varied conditions — always useful and adding a touch of elegance to their environment. Bamboo is a poignant metaphor for stewardship. They embody the characteristics of steward leadership, and reflect the essence of responsible wealth creation.

Desk Editor: Daniele Lee
Design and layout by: Loo Chuan Ming

Contents

Preface

It was the best of times, it was the worst of times, it was the age of wisdom, it was the age of foolishness, it was the epoch of belief, it was the epoch of incredulity, it was the season of Light, it was the season of Darkness, it was the spring of hope, it was the winter of despair.
— *Charles Dickens*[1]

The world has seen huge social improvement and technological progress. We have experienced unprecedented economic growth and lifted hundreds of millions of people out of poverty. We're benefiting from a life-changing digital revolution that could help solve our most pressing social and environmental challenges. Yet despite these successes, our current model of development is deeply flawed. Signs of failure and imperfections in today's markets are everywhere.
— *BSDC report 2017*[2]

Our system of wealth creation is at a major crossroads. It has contributed to social improvement, technological progress, unprecedented economic growth, better infrastructure, education, employment opportunities, as well as a life-changing digital revolution. At the same time, it has also given rise to an unstoppable demand for scarce natural resources. If left unchecked, uninhibited consumerism may fuel many problems: climate change repercussions, air pollution, modern-day slavery, digital manipulation, and invasion of one's privacy.

In its 2017 report, the Business & Sustainability Development Commission (BSDC) noted that natural disasters triggered by climate change have doubled in frequency since the 1980s. Violence and armed conflict cost the world the equivalent of 9 per cent of GDP in 2014. Lost biodiversity and ecosystem damage cost an estimated 3 per cent. Social inequality and youth unemployment are worsening in some countries around the world. On average, women are still paid 25 per cent less than men for comparable work.[3]

Some of these issues are the result of rising populations and rapid urbanisation. Megacities are becoming ever more congested. People are living longer. Artificial intelligence, robotics, medical innovation, genetic modification and many other branches of technology are changing and disrupting the way people work, play and live. Migration flows, whether driven by economic factors, ethnic conflicts, or natural disasters, give rise to social tensions. Rapid economic growth may have lifted many out of poverty, but this does not necessarily address the issue of widening economic and social disparity. Business leaders, together with consumers, and governments, bear some share of responsibility, either directly or indirectly.

By the same token, we all have a role to play in making things better. We need every ounce of human ingenuity if societies are to be set on a less damaging course in the coming years. We need the creative force of entrepreneurs, the galvanising force of forward-thinking companies, and the versatility of markets to achieve this. We would also need a better framework for the workings of the market. We need to do better at valuing the future and rewarding those whose work will benefit future generations. We need a better form of capitalism, one which, while promoting competition, is here to serve and not dominate, to respect human beings and not exploit them, to nurture our environment and not destroy it. The question is: how do we attain that?

How do we make our system of wealth creation no less adventurous, but at the same time more human, more honest, more responsible, more inclusive, more engaging, and more respectful of the needs of our grandchildren? How do business leaders, investors and policymakers create, lead and influence companies that we can all have trust in and be proud of, and thereby pave the way for a better form of capitalism, one which serves society and safeguards future generations?

In healthcare, the most long-lasting and effective help for patients is not an imposed regime or new pills. From time to time, these interventions are necessary but on their own, they are not enough. Helping sick people get well requires helping them to find the motivation within themselves to heal and not relying solely on externally prescribed regimes.

The same is true in the world of business and investment and its contribution to human well-being. Laws, rules, taxation and incentives are only part of the answer. They are the hardware of the system that channels money into productive and profitable businesses. But what about the software, or "heartware", that is the attitudes and behaviours that permeate our system of wealth creation? This is where stewardship plays its part. In this book we introduce — or, to be more accurate, reintroduce — the concept of stewardship and describe how, in practice, it has helped some organisations address the problems of capitalism and how it will continue to do so in the future by bridging the broken connections among companies, shareholders and society.

THREE ELEPHANTS

In describing stewardship over the last few years, we encountered three difficulties which we now affectionately call "our three elephants". Each of these elephants refers to a different host of issues that arise when discussing stewardship.

Elephants in the room

Firstly, there are "the elephants in the room". By this, we mean some of those well-intended and oft-repeated assumptions and solutions that people privately question but publicly accept. Having better corporate governance is an obvious example. Every time there is a corporate disaster, we are told that if only there had been better corporate governance, it could have been prevented. We were all supposed to have learnt our lesson after the global financial crisis. There is now an abundance of codes, guidelines and "comply or explain" regimes. More countries have instituted new rules, reporting requirements, and auditing standards. Company reports are now much longer and more detailed. But, have we achieved anything by doing this?

Corporate Social Responsibility (CSR) is another such "elephant". It has become a watchword for companies and a "must-have" chapter in many glossy (and maybe even integrated) annual reports. Real CSR is only achieved when a company can show that it is living its values in all its relationships.

Another elephant in the room is companies preaching their commitment to inclusivity and teamwork, while treating top management like a privileged elite, and/or considering their employees as disposable resources in the system. Shareholder activists are often lauded as champions of better corporate governance. But there are many shareholder activists who use their ownership rights to manoeuvre for short-term pay-outs, without having any interest in the long-term health of the company. Yet, few people dare to call them out for their hostility towards stewardship.

Another of these "elephants in the room" comprises two great oversimplifications. One oversimplification is the claim that capitalism can somehow be abolished and replaced by some system that does away with a market economy, choice and competition. The other opposing oversimplification is the claim that business can somehow stand outside society and ignore human purposes.

Grey elephants

Secondly, there are the "grey elephants" of stewardship. Stewardship does not represent a simple solution. It often deals with the things that are subtle and complex, that is grey, rather than black or white. This is because stewards take responsibility for all the consequences of their actions. They weigh the conflicting impact of any decision. They confront dilemmas, and a dilemma is a choice between good options, not between no-brainer alternatives. For example, the pension fund trustee has to think about the present and the future at the same time — how to achieve returns for beneficiaries today without poisoning the well from which their successors will draw future returns. And while it may be in the beneficiaries' interest for all the companies in the portfolio to prosper, that does not mean the portfolio should remain unchanged in the interest of a general commitment to the longer term. The interests of the pension fund are not the same as the interests of a particular company in the portfolio. Directors must address painful short-term necessities such as closures or relocations, while remaining consistently focused on the long-term view. The well-known "serenity prayer" goes: "Grant me the serenity to accept the things I cannot change, courage to change the things that I can, and the wisdom to know the difference." Stewardship is the wisdom that allows the company to be hard-nosed in meeting business competition while being compassionate in caring for its employees. It is the wisdom of staying true to principles while being agile in changing times.

Seven blind men touching an elephant

Thirdly, there is the elephant in the familiar parable of "seven blind men touching an elephant". In this image, each blind man touches a different part of the elephant and describes a different beast. None sees the whole. Stewardship means different things to different people. Many people recognise individual elements that constitute parts of the stewardship totality. Our task in this book is to describe the whole elephant, because stewardship is a systemic concept and its power lies in its ability to help address systemic issues. Wealth creation is a team game. Its best fruits come from the synergistic contribution of entrepreneurs, employees, managers, boards, asset managers, and asset owners.

This book is written out of a combination of experience and conviction. As co-authors, we have different backgrounds and life stories, one from the West and one from the East. One of us has worked in the UK in manufacturing, been active in politics, and founded Tomorrow's Company, an organisation with over twenty-five years of work championing the role of business as a force for good. The other has been a public servant and a leader in his country's military before taking up a corporate career working for a major state investment organisation and a utility company, starting his own consulting company, and establishing Stewardship Asia Centre. We met five years ago, and have discovered from our respective backgrounds in West and East that we are on a very similar journey of discovering the importance of stewardship, and we share the motivation to promote stewardship.

An elusive concept, stewardship has been used in different contexts. The best way to understand it is to experience it at work. In Chapter 1, we describe stewardship in action in different parts of the world, and set the stage for what will follow by examining some of the debates and assumptions that underpin our wealth-creation system.

With this as a backdrop, Chapter 2 defines and describes stewardship. It sets out three elements (will, time connectivity and interdependence) and five core concepts (ownership, purpose, long-term view, relationships and community). These elements and concepts form the framework for the subsequent discussion of stewardship.

Chapter 3 describes the role of organisational leaders as stewards. A stewardship approach in leading the organisation can be seen as a virtuous circle. It helps companies find the individual identity that leads to ownership commitment. It also achieves the alignment of purpose and values, and prioritises wider societal and community relationships. Leaders who practise stewardship identify key relationships, including the vital relationship with the community and society from which the company originated. They define what they mean by success and value. They are clear about time horizons. They observe a balance between performance and behaviour. They measure long-term value as well as short-term performance. They develop an ownership mentality and reward stewardship behaviour. They take an integrated approach to the measurement and communication of the company's performance and impact. They learn from feedback and adapt. They lead with impact, safeguard the future and drive social good.

Chapter 4 describes all the links and accountabilities that connect savers and investors (including intermediaries) with companies and their boards. We call this the stewardship value chain. Stewardship is the joint responsibility of the owners and the board. Each of the actors along the value chain can contribute, as a steward, to responsible wealth creation and act in ways that are aligned with the ideals of better capitalism. We consider the often-misunderstood term fiduciary duty and describe its role for both institutional investors and boards.

Chapter 5 discusses the role of the board as steward. Directors of a company are entrusted by owners, investors and shareholders with the care of the business. To fulfil its fiduciary duty, the board needs to observe four stewardship priorities: establishing a mandate, continuously improving qualitative and quantitative outcomes, sensing and shaping the external landscape, and balancing present and future needs. In the present climate of short-termism, balancing both present and future needs will require commitment and courage.

Chapter 6 considers the role of asset owners and asset managers in serving their ultimate clients and beneficiaries, and points out the frequent failure of asset managers in identifying the value that their clients and beneficiaries want. Shareholders are ultimately citizens and this influences how they see value. The clients of asset managers need the opportunity to steer asset managers towards strategies that promote long-term wealth creation. This chapter offers the stewardship criteria for assessing asset owners and an agenda for institutional investors.

Chapter 7 outlines the role of the state as steward. Governments can and do play multiple and varied roles through various mechanisms and structures, particularly as regulators, asset owners, and asset managers, all key components of responsible wealth creation. Creating a conducive environment that promotes wealth creation responsibly is critical to the process of gaining or regaining trust for businesses to thrive. This chapter will delve into examples of policies that can facilitate stewardship at different levels, and the contribution of the state as a steward in its role as an asset owner in business.

Rounding it up, Chapter 8 explores the role of stewardship in fostering a better capitalism that can serve the human purposes of business, both now and in the future. Through examining the paradoxes that pervade our lives, we call for a better alignment between the operation of markets and the needs of society. This can be achieved by interweaving the thread of stewardship throughout the whole value creation process.

Chapter 1

(Re)Discovering Stewardship

We believe business can be, and must be, a force
for good; and we believe the challenges the world
faces are best served through harnessing business'
resolve, creativity and resources.
— *Tomorrow's Company*[1]

Imagine a family business thriving for over 46 generations — a period lasting over 1300 years.

Or a global company which recovered from a devastating scandal to become an acknowledged leader in sustainability.

Or a company which survived serious fragmentation of its ownership structure and re-emerging united and resilient.

Or a burgeoning hospitality business which succeeded by creating a lush paradise out of a mining wasteland.

Or a young consumer goods company whose CEO and employees took sledgehammers to defective products, which has now become recognised for the high quality of its goods.

What do these diverse companies have in common? What differentiates them from others? The answer: stewardship. In each of these cases, the company concerned has imbibed and practised the spirit of stewardship. In each example, stewardship has been essential for the company's success. These companies exemplify

1

stewardship in action, each in its own prevailing business landscape. Read this chapter and the next for a snapshot of these well-stewarded companies.

A GLIMPSE OF STEWARDSHIP IN ACTION

Consider a 1300-year-old company, which operates the world's second-oldest hotel, *Hoshi Ryokan.* Founded in 718, this Japanese family-run business has flourished for forty-six generations. The Hoshi family is not only a steward of its business, but a steward of local heritage too. The inn draws its life force from the Awazu hot spring that has flowed continuously for over a millennium. Legend has it that a Buddhist priest unearthed the hot spring after he received a sacred message from a deity. His disciple then built an inn over its site and used the healing water to serve the community. Says Zengoro Hoshi, the current patriarch: "The Hoshi family's responsibilities are in passing on our long history for future generations and to protect our hot spring."[2] The family has not only grown the inn business over the years, but as part of the company's conservation efforts, the inn makes a point of caring for the precious gift from nature. As Hoshi puts it:

> Nothing has ever belonged to me. I believe the key for continuity and long-term prosperity is to maintain inherited assets as if they are not my own properties. They are just temporary under my management and governance. Thus, understanding this mission, we have to work hard to grow the value and assets, in both quantitative and qualitative terms.[3]

Coupled with its philosophy of "less greed and realisation of enough", the family mindfully seeks to maintain the delicate balance between the needs of *business, community and environment*.[4]

Also in Asia, the Chinese firm Haier made headlines in 2016 when it acquired General Electric's (GE) appliance unit with a hefty US$5.4 billion price tag,[5] a turn of the tide considering the fact that the century-old conglomerate had once wanted to take over Haier in a failed attempt in the early 1990s.[6] Back in the 1980s, Haier was a manufacturing company of small, poor-quality fridges. One in five of their manufactured fridges were found to be faulty. In a landmark move in 1985, the founder, Zhang Ruimin gathered workers and joined them in smashing seventy-six malfunctioning fridges with sledgehammers, sending a strong signal that the company would not eschew quality.[7] Today, it has become one of the major global players in the field.[8] According to the founder, the success of the company hinges on the persistent adoption of a people-centric approach.[9] The company links employees' performance to how well they are connected to customers, especially in terms of creating and adding value for them. To further enhance value creation, the founder turned the business into an open network. Employees with novel ideas can now become entrepreneurs, setting up micro enterprises within Haier. This structure allows employees to respond to the evolving demands of customers in a nimbler way. Zhang's success in creating a deep *culture of ownership* among the employees in Haier has transformed the company over three decades. Across the globe, many other organisations from different sectors have adopted the model with success, underscoring the transferability of this approach across cultures.[10]

Purpose and values play an important part in steering the direction of companies. Firms that are driven by purpose and anchored on values are more likely to overcome and bounce back from a crisis. Siemens, one of the world's largest electrical companies, based in Germany, is an example. So effectively did it steward itself out of a global bribery scandal (uncovered in 2006) that by 2018, it was being recognised as one of the world's top companies for sustainability.[11] Charged with attempting to increase market share through corrupt practices, Siemens paid more than US$1.6 billion in fines in multiple countries in 2008. In the aftermath of the scandal, the company reset its *purpose and values* and established an environmental portfolio to track products that were energy- and resource-efficient.[12] This further developed into identifying "sustainable development as the means to achieve profitable and long-term growth", setting the stage for the company to practise one of the core stewardship traits of having a *long-term focus*.[13] Aligning its interests with the United Nations Sustainable Development Goals (SDGs), the company has since committed to cutting its global carbon imprint in half by 2020 and making its operations carbon neutral by 2030. It has focused on innovation as well as research and development (R&D) to meet its goals.

Beyond changing societal norms, some companies also link the higher purpose of their existence to national development. Founded 186 years ago, and now in its eighth generation of leadership, Ayala Corporation is one of the leading and oldest industrial conglomerates in the Philippines. In 1997, Ayala signed a water concession agreement to operate the water and sewer systems of Metro Manila's east zone.[14] Its CEO, Jaime Augusto Zobel de Ayala, felt that "proper water management was critical for the economic development of Manila" and saw an opportunity for Ayala to contribute to nation-building.[15] He said:

As we moved into the year 2000, the Ayala Group that I represented was really dealing with the top end of the market. And I asked, how do we grow and how (are) we to be relevant in our society if we don't start to address the needs of the greater mass of customers in the Philippines that were at a whole different price point? We have to transform our business model to become relevant to a greater percentage of our population. We moved into infrastructure, water distribution and the like, that started to deal with communities at whole different price points, and we had to change all our business models to adjust to that world. We created, I like to think, a philosophy of inclusiveness that fundamentally changed our business model, changed the trust that was developed with that customer base and really built a lot of goodwill with the communities that we were serving, just by beginning to adjust to those needs.[16]

Such a move is aligned with the founder's aspirations. From the outset, Ayala's founder Antonio de Ayala emphasised the importance of being a steward to ensure the success of the company and all its stakeholders.[17] From generation to generation, the spirit of stewardship has been passed down to succeeding leadership and the company as a whole. In 2014, Ayala was awarded the prestigious IMD-Lombard Odier Global Family Business Network International (FBN-I) award, an award that "celebrates the impact of family-run firms on the global economy".[18] In essence, the corporation was recognised for its "strongly rooted values; long-term, strategic partnerships; commitment to family leadership and stewardship; consistency of values across generations; contribution to the nation's development and its integration into the family's long term business interest; and well-planned succession policies".[19] Ayala is one example of a well-stewarded company that flourishes by consistently looking to create "purpose [and value] beyond just making money".[20]

Similarly, state-owned entities can model the way for actualising long-termism and fulfilling a purpose beyond just making money. Established in 1974 and wholly owned by Singapore's Ministry of Finance, Temasek Holdings is the Republic's state investment company with an internationally diversified portfolio. By 2018, it had achieved a net portfolio value of US$235 billion and enjoyed an annualised total shareholder return of 15 per cent since its inception.[21] Over the years, the organisation has been maintaining its strong credit ratings from both Moody's and S&P, indicating a stable outlook that is tied to its prudent and conservative approach to investment and funding strategy.[22] As articulated by Ho Ching, CEO of Temasek Holdings, the organisation "looks beyond the narrow confines of profits" and is committed to doing well as an investor, doing right as an institution and doing good as a steward. Guided by an ethos of sustainability and good governance, Temasek adopts a long-term horizon for its investment activities.[23] It is constantly reshaping its portfolio for sustainable long-term returns to deliver for future generations,[24] and its returns are generally retained for reinvestment.[25] Temasek defines in its Charter its goal to be an active investor, a long-term institution and a trusted steward. Those are words that Temasek lives by. Chairman of Temasek Holdings, Lim Boon Heng, says:

> To succeed as an investor is not an end in itself. Ultimately, that success must be translated into a better and more sustainable world, with more opportunities, and a kinder place for people and communities.[26]

To fulfil the role of being a steward of the community as well as of future generations, Temasek Holdings has established a family of foundations and endowments to build people, capabilities and communities, both within and beyond the shores of Singapore.

These five examples provide glimpses into how businesses can steward themselves towards success and longevity in a purposeful manner, impacting communities beyond themselves. All five companies have a clear sense of purpose that goes beyond profit. They look beyond their immediate self-interest. They integrate the interests of the environment and the wider community with their business models. They show an understanding of interdependence among businesses, societies and the world at large. They also invest in relationships and build on them for future growth. Whether in calm or crisis conditions, these companies value enduring relationships. These companies, and others like them, are part of a growing momentum of businesses that understand, practise and live stewardship.

By their example and their track record, these businesses represent a living challenge to the assumptions that have too often been made about capitalism and the motivations of those who work in the capitalist system. Before going on to Chapter 2, it is worth reflecting on what those assumptions are and where they have led, or often misled us. We then explain how the stewardship view of a company compares with two competing views, which are shareholder primacy, and stakeholder theory.

STARTING WITH THE MIND

What is the purpose of business? Is it to serve customers, to make money for shareholders, to create employment, to solve society's problems, to make a few entrepreneurs rich, or to benefit future generations? There are debates about this. These debates can be broken down into five key differences in opinion about the nature of business.

Motivation — Money or More

The first question is: *what motivates people in business?*

At one end of the spectrum is a mindset that assumes that people are motivated only by money and that all their decision-making can be explained by this motivation. This thinking could arguably be traced back to economists' well-meaning construct of an imaginary person called *Homo Economicus*. By definition, this economic man is only interested in financial incentives, financial measures and financial results. He was invented to help economists explain how the market works, and to test some theories meant to predict what happens in the economic world. This is necessary for, say, calculating the response of consumers to changes in prices. In constructing economic man, economists did not claim that this is a complete description or accurate depiction of how most people make decisions. Nor did they claim that people were always rational when they made their decisions.

At the other end of the spectrum, motivation is seen as much more mixed and complicated. There is a hierarchy of needs, and motivation changes as the more basic needs are met. People who work in organisations need money, but they also need a sense of belonging, pride and achievement. Buying decisions are often influenced by emotion.

Markets — Master or Servant

The second question is: *how much do business people trust markets for the right answer?*

On one side are the market disciples who believe that markets are generally right, that you can rely on market forces and that markets do not lie. They believe that market mechanisms are "self-healing". These market disciples prefer to let the market find the answer without regulatory interference.

On the other side, however, are those who say that this is a naive belief, which, among many things, ignores the effect of herding behaviours which have shown up in every market since the Dutch went mad about tulips in the seventeenth century. The same behaviours could be seen in the build-up to the 2008 financial crisis. It took major government intervention, and not the self-healing power of markets, to prevent a disastrous crash. In this view, market forces have to be harnessed.

Business — Part of or Apart from Society

The third question is: *how do people see the relationship between business and society?*

On one side, business and society sit in separate compartments. Businesses should not worry about the needs of society, but focus on profits. It is not productive for business to "take its eye off the ball" and concern itself with the needs of society. The only responsibility of a business is to make a profit. The "invisible hand" of the market ensures that the pursuit of profit by individuals is of benefit to society. Adam Smith's "invisible hand" is often quoted in support of the compartmentalised view of business and society. He used the "invisible hand" to explain how the operation of the market under the efficient division of labour would serve to align the self-interest of individuals to the well-being of all. In doing so, Smith however made a crucial assumption, which is that the market operates within the norms of a civilised society in which people know how they ought to behave for the wider benefit of all. As he puts it:

> How selfish soever man may be supposed, there are inevitably some principles in his nature, which interest him in the fortune of others, and render their happiness necessary to him, though he derives nothing from it except the pleasure of seeing it.[27]

Contrast Smith's nuanced approach with the crude championing of businesses' self-interest, as embodied by the fictional character Gordon Gekko in the Hollywood classic *Wall Street*. Gekko says: "Greed is good. Greed is right. Greed works. Greed clarifies, cuts through and captures the essence of the evolutionary spirit. Greed, in all of its forms, greed for life, for money, for love, knowledge, has marked the upward surge of mankind."[28] Real-life Gekkos see business as being apart from society, operating in its own moral vacuum, somehow exonerated by the mystical powers of market forces from examining the consequences of its actions.

On the other side of this argument is the belief that business is a part of society, not apart from it. Business activity feeds on the capital that society and nature provide, and in return, businesses offer society its constant innovation, and the chance to raise living standards, communication, travel and entertainment.

Value — Scarce or Abundant

The fourth question is: *how do people in business see value? Do they think in terms of abundance or scarcity?*

Some people see business in narrow financial terms. Business is about making money. They think of business as a zero-sum game. Spending more than what the market requires on workers' wages, investing more in the community, or giving more to charity, means having less left for shareholder returns. Milton Friedman's famous 1970 article on social responsibility has been interpreted as exemplifying this zero-sum game perspective:

> There is one and only one social responsibility of business — to use its resources and engage in activities designed to increase its profits so long as it stays within the rules of the game, which is to say, engages in open and free competition, without deception or fraud.[29]

Those who see business as a zero-sum game may not see the possibility of managers wanting their businesses to make profits for shareholders while being a force for good.

In contrast, many in business are seeing value as a positive-sum game. For them, the best of companies create value in ways that are a win-win for shareholders, other stakeholders, and society.

People — Whole or In Part

The fifth question is: *how do people think about shareholders and other stakeholders?*

Do they see shareholders, customers, suppliers, workers, and citizens as distinct and separate groups of people, each with their own common interest? Or do they view terms like "shareholder" and "stakeholder" as descriptions of a particular role that people may have in one particular situation?

To some, people can and do have multiple roles. For instance, when you shop in a supermarket, you are a customer. But you may also be a shareholder indirectly through a life insurance policy or a pension fund. Conversely, when you own shares in a company, you may be more than a shareholder if you are also a customer of its product, a member of the society affected by the company's pollution, or beneficiary of its contribution to the community. Once it becomes obvious that people have multiple roles, the insistence that companies should be organised exclusively around the pursuit of *shareholder value* begins to seem less logical.

The responses to the five questions could be broadly divided into two approaches: an inclusive approach and an exclusive approach.

An *exclusive approach* tends to narrow issues to simple, either/ or answers. It starts with the assumptions of "homo economicus" and works on the basis that money is what motivates people. It cuts business off from considerations of its responsibilities to society. It shows a strong faith in market signals. It ignores the fact that people do wear different hats at different moments.

An *inclusive approach*, by contrast, sees people as being partly motivated by money, but also by other things as well. It sees their self-interest as enlightened self-interest, tinged by a sense of responsibility to others. It sees value in terms of abundance, not scarcity, and looks for "win-win" so that more value for one stakeholder does not necessarily mean less for another. It sees markets, profits and shareholder value as a useful servant but a bad master — they are means and not ends. Likewise, it sees finance as an instrument of wealth creation, a part of economic life, not as an end in itself.

An inclusive approach is complex and more subtle. It acknowledges interdependence, seeing businesses as living systems which have their own unique purpose and values. The Chinese phrase for business is 生意 (sheng yi), comprising two words denoting "life" and "meaning", underscoring that business is a living entity that is purposeful. Business is a part of society, and society is a subset of the natural environment. All are interdependent parts of a larger system, and the human person is part of the community around it. An inclusive approach sees the investment system as being dynamic in nature, which needs to be judged not by some abstract market criterion but by how well it contributes to a growing system of wealth creation within a healthy society.

This inclusive approach to the nature of business can be found at the heart of a stewardship mindset. Pulling all the five strands together, *a stewardship mindset* reflects the following key ideas:

- People are interested in profit, but are motivated by more than just money

- Business, finance and markets should be seen as servants, and not masters

- Business is a part of society, not apart from it

- Neither market forces, nor imposed regulations, will deliver the right outcomes for society on their own. Without the enlightened self-interest of responsible entrepreneurs and wealth creators, any market system will degenerate into a see-saw between greed and bureaucracy

- Business is conducted to meet human and social needs, and should be judged by the total value it creates in contributing to human well-being, of which financial value is one part

THREE VIEWS OF THE COMPANY

Conventional answers to the question "What is the purpose of business?" tend to be divided into two opposing camps. The stewardship mindset offers a third way of answering the question.

Shareholder primacy and stakeholder theory

In late-2017, Paul Polman announced his intention to step down as CEO of Unilever, one of the world's most successful and enduring listed companies. This sparked a wealth of conflicting comments about his decade of leadership. The Lex Column in London's *Financial Times* has always tended to reflect the views of institutional shareholders and investment bankers, and it commented that "he [Polman] went on too much about sustainability for many people's liking".[30] This is the view of the world that tends to prevail in financial centres, wherever shares of listed companies are traded. There, people see the company as a purely financial entity. The company is analysed as if it were no more than a piece of property belonging to its shareholders. They can do with it what they will. If it is a listed company, they can trade its shares or force it into liquidation. They can demand that it increase the dividend, or pay them handsome share buybacks without regard for its ability to invest. The board of directors are their agents, there to do their bidding in order to secure the fullest financial returns. Shareholder interests take priority, and that means the shareholders today. If a new activist shareholder buys enough shares, the company can be expected to change course. The job of the CEO and senior management is to crank the handle and make sure the cash keeps flowing. This is what is usually described as shareholder primacy.

The second view is, in many ways, the mirror image of the first. Under this view, the board's job is to balance the interests of many stakeholders, such as customers, employees, suppliers, the community in its various forms, and of course, shareholders. The logic here is that relationships are crucial to the success of the company. For the company to be successful, it has to create value for customers and employees. If it has poor relationships with suppliers or the community, not only will they suffer, but so will shareholders. Moreover, under this view, the success of the company cannot be measured in financial terms alone. Under some jurisdictions, for example, Germany, the stakeholder approach is underpinned by a two-tier board structure and a form of co-partnership. The Supervisory Board is elected or nominated by different constituencies so that it can truly represent the interests that need to be served by the company.

Under stakeholder theory, the company is not a bundle of contracts. It is a bundle of relationships. It amounts to much more than just a shareholder's plaything. It is a social as well as an economic institution. Even if the board does not formally include stakeholder representatives, it has both a need and an obligation to treat stakeholders decently and make appropriate balances between their claims.

Comparing the two views

The main advantage of shareholder primacy is its simplicity: shareholders come first, period. There are no arguments, except when different shareholders cannot agree. The main advantage of the stakeholder theory is its focus on the importance of relationships. However, the problem about both shareholder primacy and stakeholder theory is that, in different ways, they emphasise conflicts rather than search for a community of interest. Shareholder primacy does it by giving shareholders dominance. Stakeholder theory leads to stakeholder-friendly governance, reporting and consultation obligations. These may increase the legitimacy of decision-making but can very easily slow the entrepreneurial pace of the organisation. Shareholder primacy has some form of linear logic to it. Stakeholder theory can leave businesses with a spaghetti of different accountabilities. There are also difficulties with both views when it comes to the question of how success is to be measured and reported. The apparent simplicity of the shareholder primacy approach leaves it open to manipulation. If profit is the only criterion for judging the success of a company, then profit can get manipulated. If the company is judged on share price performance, then the temptation is for its leaders to spend their lives worrying about keeping the current share price high, rather than focusing on the steps that will ensure the future success of the company. If the pay of senior executives depends on share price performance, then that focus can become an obsession. The stakeholder theory approach can also have its difficulties with measurement. Shareholder primacy keeps things simple by focusing on financial performance and benefits to shareholders. A stakeholder theory approach opens the door to measuring and reporting every single variable that stakeholders may feel to be important. In the process, there is a risk that people can no longer understand the story the company is telling.

A stewardship view

It makes sense, therefore, to put the focus on the success of the company and the achievement of its purpose. The focus is not on the rights or claims of any group involved with the company but on the success of the company in the long term. This view, which is what stewardship represents, offers the best of both worlds, combining respect for the importance of relationships with the freedom for businesses to move fast. It does not put shareholders first or even all stakeholders first. It puts the success of the company first. It is the view that is to be found among owners of long-lived family businesses who have a natural desire to pass on the company and its assets, relationships, and values in a better condition than they inherited them.

In this view, directors are elected by shareholders and are, in formal terms, unambiguously accountable to them. But they owe their *duty* to the company, not to shareholders and stakeholders. Their duty is to promote the success of the company. They have been entrusted by shareholders (who are often intermediaries who have in turn been entrusted by the ultimate beneficiaries) with the responsibility to take care of and grow the assets of the company so that when it is time to hand on to the successors, the company is in the best possible condition. They achieve returns for shareholders by using their judgement about how the success of the company is best achieved. Equally, they achieve benefits for society and the other stakeholders by recognising that relationships are the key to success. There is a presumption that the board needs to balance the claims of the short term with those of the long term.

It is no coincidence that the stewardship view of the company works most naturally where ownership is more concentrated. In addition to long-standing family businesses, stewardship can flourish in businesses owned and controlled by trusts or foundations, or by responsible state-owners of long-term businesses who see beyond the short-term nature of projects and possess a strong sense of purpose to create wealth and better conditions for the larger community, across generations. They know that they will best serve the interests of owners, employees and other stakeholders if they place the company's success and its present and future well-being first.

Table 1: Three Views of the Company

Three Views of the Company	Shareholder Primacy	Stakeholder Theory	Stewardship Actions
Directors are	Agents	Representatives	Stewards
Promoting success of	Today's shareholders	Shareholders and stakeholders	The company and thereby today's and tomorrow's shareholders and stakeholders
Formally accountable to	Today's shareholders	Whoever nominated or elected them	Shareholders (not simply the asset managers but including the ultimate owners)
Success is seen as	Share price and shareholder value	Triple bottom line: Economic, Social and Environmental	Delivering value to owners and stakeholders through the company's long-term success
Measured over	Quarters	Short, medium and long term	Short, medium and long term
Reported through	Financial accounts	Global Reporting Initiative etc.	Integrated Reports
The company is	The property of the shareholders	Social as well as financial institution	A living entity whose success depends on entrepreneurial flair and its relationships

Note: We employ some oversimplification and overstate the differences between the three views of the company so as to highlight the key differences between each viewpoint.

Chapter 2

Understanding Stewardship

THE ELEMENTS OF STEWARDSHIP

Stewardship is the "responsible and wholehearted management of entrusted assets so as to pass them on in better condition". It contains three elements. Stewardship starts with the will of the individual; stewardship connects past, present and future; and stewardship is about interdependence.

Stewardship is a matter of will

The first element is all about the will, that is, individual commitment and personal motivation. Stewardship is about moving from "I should" to "I will". A steward is there to protect and enhance value for others. It is not enough just to fulfil obligations as an agent — to simply take a percentage of the assets being managed, comply with a set of legally specified obligations, and ride comfortably along. Value is likely to be lost when assets are managed by people with such an agent mentality. Agents do not see themselves as long-term owners. They do not think like owners. But stewards have an ownership mentality, and it is a commitment driven by will. Stewardship means a sense of responsibility that goes beyond an adherence to imposed rules. For a board of directors thinking about corporate governance, the question should not be "Are we complying with this requirement or code?" but "Are we living up to our purpose and our principles?" The same applies to the trustees of a pension fund, asset managers, or the directors of an insurance company. This element of stewardship echoes Mahatma Gandhi's ethos: we must be the change we wish to see in the world.[1] Li Rong Rong, the first chairman of China's SASAC (State-owned Assets Supervision and Administration Commission) described the motivational element of stewardship by interchanging the position of two characters of a Chinese phase, from "要我尽责" to "我要尽责", fundamentally altering the meaning from a compliance-based corporate governance to self-willed stewardship. The steward emphasises "I will" rather than "I should". The "will" makes all the difference between compliance and commitment, change and transformation, the letter and the spirit. Stewardship is concerned with values beyond rules; effects and not box-ticking; impact rather than output; action and not only words; commitment beyond just involvement; and leadership, not position.

Stewardship connects the past, present and the future

The second element introduces the dimension and connectedness of time. It builds on the steward's personal motivation to fulfil his or her responsibilities and places it squarely in an intergenerational context. Those who are entrusted with assets and responsibilities have an obligation to care and grow them over time. Stewardship motivates each of us to discharge our responsibilities and pass the baton well to successors or the next generation. The assets for which a steward has become responsible have been built up by predecessors and need to be sustained by successors, on behalf of the beneficiaries. Stewardship involves a sense of legacy from the past and responsibility for the future. Across cultures, there is a common belief that we have a responsibility, to our fellow human beings and across generations, just as a Chinese proverb urges one generation to plant trees, so that the next generation can enjoy the shade (前人栽树、后人乘凉). The role of the steward is about preserving and enhancing value over time, on behalf of others to come.

Stewardship is about interdependence

The third element is a recognition that stewardship is about creating value and wealth in an interdependent manner. Stewards acknowledge and celebrate interdependence. In order to fulfil stewardship intent, the steward focuses on effective relationships in all the activities that are key to protecting and enhancing value. The steward approaches relationships in a spirit of abundance, not scarcity. The steward looks beyond minimum obligations to stakeholders and seeks to promote reciprocity. That means ensuring that, wherever it is practicable, all parties benefit in the longer term from a deal. Stewards go the extra mile in their conduct of all relationships upon which the protection or the creation of value depends. It means checking that others who are part of the value chain are truly living up to its intentions, fulfilling expectations in spirit as well as in letter, and not merely complying with technical requirements. Some businesses enjoy a relatively short value chain, such as family businesses, employee-owned businesses, mutuals and state-owned businesses. For others, the chain stretches so far that recipients of funds can feel no connection with the original providers of those funds. At one end, there is the individual saver or investor. Savings flow through the hands of a succession of intermediaries and end up in the hands of an asset manager. At the other end of the chain is the user of funds. This may be an entrepreneur seeking finance to grow a business, a private company backed by private equity finance, or a listed company with dispersed shareholding. The greater the length of the chain, the more important it is to keep this third stewardship element alive. What matters here is the acknowledgement that stewardship only works where full attention is given to relationships, and the obligations and opportunities that they represent.

Reflecting on all three stewardship elements, the critical question facing a company is:

> How can a business thrive and sustain growth while enhancing the wealth of its stakeholders and the well-being of society in the long term?

Applying to each of us personally, stewardship is all about:

> How each of us who is entrusted with responsibilities has the motivation to fulfil them such that we can hand over what we have received in better shape?

STEWARDSHIP CORE CONCEPTS

Let us delve into the core concepts that lie at the heart of stewardship. These concepts represent the answer to the question "what causes some companies to be successful and lasting?" If you come across a well-stewarded company, you are likely to see the *manifestation* of these core concepts. In other words, if stewardship seems abstract, look instead for the presence and effects of these core concepts. If you find them, you will know that stewardship is in action.

In Japan, there are over 20,000 companies which are over 100 years old. There are 600 companies which have been successfully performing over a span of 300 years. There are 30 companies which have thrived for over 500 years. There are 5 companies which have a legacy and history of over 1,000 years. In his book *Timeless Ventures*, Professor Haruo Funabashi describes the history of 32 Japanese companies which have existed for 200 to 1,400 years.[2] From this research, he distilled eight principles essential to enduring corporate success. See Box 1 below for a synopsis of the principles.[3]

TIMELESS VENTURES – EIGHT PRINCIPLES FROM FUNABASHI'S STUDY OF 32 LONG-LIVED JAPANESE COMPANIES

1. Leadership driven by clear values, vision and mission
Funabashi found a common pattern where leadership is driven by clear values. This then provides a vision which serves two purposes: Firstly, "it triggers aspirations, motivation, meaning and purpose for all concerned".[4] Secondly, it gives a sense of direction "to translate intent into *mission for action*".[5] These companies crystallised their founders' thoughts through precepts, rules and codes of conduct, which helped to guide everyone through difficult periods.

2. Long-term viewpoint and strategic approach
This principle reflects the uniqueness of the Japanese approach. "It is about farsightedness and a vision for the long-term that secures the future".[6] It is also about "the capacity to comprehend, include and achieve something beyond the bottom line, something meaningful and ultimately worthwhile".[7] To look for a higher purpose is deeply rooted in the Japanese mindset.

3. The importance of people and human merit systems
The third factor is respecting and valuing people. "While business is certainly about making money, it is even more about having great people" to run companies.[8] Companies will be able to achieve a more enduring form of success if they are committed to education, skill-building and all-round development of their employees. In addition, enlightened business people "truly acknowledge individual identity in the bigger picture of generating teams at work. The whole idea is about putting people first".[9]

4. Customer oriented and building the economy
"No matter what business you are in, it is impossible to go on without respect for your customer."[10] Present in the long-established companies are customs and organisational routines that have been put in place to constantly remind its employees about this principle.

5. Socially minded and building the nation
This principle is derived from the belief that corporations exist to serve the society and the nation, instead of serving the self or some individual. "It reinforces the wisdom that a company exists because of society. So, a company is designed to create lasting benefits for society to create gratitude. And then it is the trust it builds in the system over the years through the magnanimity towards others such as consumers, business partners, employees and shareholders that blessings will naturally come back to it."[11]

6. Continuous innovation and improvement
"It is important to learn how to change when one must. There can be no society without change. The problem is how you can anticipate, prepare and adapt to changes by self-development and destruction (let go)."[12] Nonetheless, a business must take care not to lose its distinctiveness and competitive edge in its attempt to adapt to change.

7. Frugality and use of natural resources.
"Among Japanese people to be frugal and moderate in consumption is considered a virtue."[13] Today frugality means finding new ways to use natural resources more efficiently to make a sustainable world.

> ### 8. *Embody and generate culture/legacy*
> One of the most important traits of enduring companies is that they imbibe the previous seven principles and translate them into an organisational culture and legacy. To internalise these principles, it is important to integrate them into daily practices through "practice, procedures, protocol and ritual".[14] Leaders work to "consciously leave fond institutional memories through their actions and a personality footprint that inspire generations thereafter".[15]

Box 1: Funabashi's principles essential to the building of enduring corporate success

A recent piece of research by Tomorrow's Company explored the relationship between the constancy of company purpose and the increasing inconsistency of the surrounding world.[16] It was based on interviews with two types of companies — recently established businesses exploiting opportunities in the digital age, and long-established companies adapting to the new digital world. The research drew attention to the greater resilience of companies which have a focus on purpose beyond profit and relationships guided by clear values. It concluded that a firm and enduring purpose beyond profit is, more than ever, the precondition for true agility in the age of uncertainty. It also found that companies with a purpose beyond profit enjoyed four potential advantages in the face of change and uncertainty. Firstly, their purpose and values become a source of energy in workplace relationships, enabling them to attract and retain talent, and better engage and develop their own people. Secondly, a clear purpose, which people can naturally identify as a keel, confers stability and resilience. Strong values provide a clear basis for building trust. Thirdly, the benefits in terms of trust yield a reputational return, enhancing brands and accumulating external trust and goodwill. As a result, the licence to operate is enhanced. Fourthly, because of the first three benefits, there is a more compelling case to take to investors who are interested in long-term performance. This in turn provides a basis for building greater investor confidence which is a further source of stability for the company.

In the same vein, a recent study by Stewardship Asia Centre surveyed 200 successful and enduring companies across Asia, firms that had experienced at least one generational change and reached a proven level of profitability.[17] The study established seven common traits that have allowed such organisations to endure over generations, despite facing significant challenges in geopolitics and disruptive technologies. Ranked high on the list are: leadership, purpose, long-term vision and relationships. Looking to the future, leaders of successful and enduring companies are realistically certain that they will face tough times and crises. But they are, at the same time, cautiously confident that they will overcome and prevail, basing their optimism on successfully building up their capacity in sound leadership, a sense of purpose and values, as well as long-term planning and stable relationships. They strongly believe that leadership has to be the progenitor of the stewardship spirit and stewardship traits in the organisation. The study identified three important characteristics of the leadership of such successful and enduring companies. Firstly, strong steward leaders are those who are anchored on purpose and values. Secondly, in their pursuit of profitability, they are more likely to emphasise the needs and importance of stakeholders, and not see their interests as secondary. Thirdly, these leaders have a long-term outlook. Among these traits, having a clear, well-articulated purpose distinguishes leaders as much as it differentiates companies.

To summarise the common conclusions distilled from research, stewardship embodies these five core concepts: *ownership, purpose, long-term view, relationships and community.*

Ownership

It seems easy to speak of stewardship in theory, but people who run businesses often say, "In the real world, we have to worry about our shareholders, the owners, and they are only interested in earnings and dividends". Therefore, we need to think much harder about the role and the meaning of owners. Who are the owners? What is ownership? What does it mean to own anything? Is ownership concerned only with rights and benefits? Does it not also involve responsibility and obligations? How is ownership linked with stewardship?

The origins of the English words "to own" are the same as that of "to owe". To own something originally meant to acknowledge it as both your asset and your responsibility. Over the years, ownership has, however, become a more complex concept. If we think of the objects we "own", do we think about the rights or the responsibilities in relation to them? Let us consider a person who found himself inheriting, say, a hotel with employees dependent on it for their livelihood. He owns the asset, and with that, there are benefits and rights that come with ownership. But there is also the obligation to pass on the asset to the next generation in a better state than he had inherited it. In other words, he has become a steward. Very quickly, he would have learnt from the situation that ownership is not just about rights. Ownership clearly involves obligations and may also be burdensome.

A related term comes to mind: trusteeship. Stewardship and trusteeship are closely intertwined. Trusteeship has its origins in a formal set of legal arrangements. It involves defining the obligations of those who are responsible for an asset, and the beneficiaries to whom they owe those obligations. Stewardship, on the other hand, is not a legal concept. But both terms embody the same idea, that all those who are entrusted with assets have an obligation to look after those assets. For both stewardship and trusteeship, once again, ownership is not just about rights. Owning something involves obligations.

In a simple value chain, we have shareholders on one side, and they are the owners of the business. On the other side are the board directors and managers of the business. They are not the asset owners, but are the stewards entrusted to manage and grow those assets. Though it may sound paradoxical, it is important to understand that "owners should have a stewardship mentality, and stewards should have an ownership mentality", because they are two sides of the same coin. Stewardship for the owners means they are motivated to think and act as though they do not really own the asset, but are looking after it and growing it, for the next generation. What this means is that though they are indeed the owner, they care for the asset with a stewardship mentality. Conversely, for the stewards of the company like the directors and managers, they are entrusted by the owners to run and grow the company. They should thus operate with an ownership mentality, discharging their obligations as though they themselves own the asset.

Companies which aspire to continue their life and work over many decades need the stability of ownership. If the owners are interested only in what they can extract in dividends and capital gains over a few years, then they must expect to live with the consequences of their choices. Nowhere in the catalogue of companies with a record of enduring success over generations can we find transactional companies that see themselves only as "earnings machines". A successful and enduring business needs to be anchored by long-term owners who see themselves as stewards of the asset with which they have been entrusted.

Take the case of Eu Yan Sang. Founded in 1879, Eu Yan Sang is a 140-year-old global healthcare and wellness company with a strong foundation in Traditional Chinese Medicine (TCM). In Asia, it is a household name and leader in its field. Driven by the purpose of "benevolence and life" (as its name Yan Sang, 仁生, means), Eu Yan Sang was established with the intent of providing Chinese herbal remedies for ailing workers as an alternative to opium. Till today, it remains committed to providing quality care for patients and continues to gain a strong foothold in the market through its holistic suite of products. Headquartered in Singapore, the family business is now in its fourth generation of leadership, breaking the curse of "from shirtsleeves to shirtsleeves in three generations". It currently runs more than 230 retail outlets in Hong Kong, Macau, China, Malaysia, Singapore and Australia, and operates thirty TCM clinics in Asia.[18]

Its path towards success, however, has been tumultuous. Eu Tong Sen, a second-generation leader, took over the helm of the family business following the sudden demise of his father, Eu Kong, who passed away at thirty-eight. Upon the tycoon's death, the family business was distributed among his thirteen sons. This became the catalyst for discordant family relations and turmoil. Although the Eu family had dominant ownership and control of the company, most of the third-generation members did not actively participate in the management. Trusted employees managed the business instead.[19] In 1973, Eu Yan Sang became a listed company.[20] Things took a precarious turn in 1990 when fragmented ownership and differences in interests among family members led to several ventures being sold off to an external party, the Lum Chang Group.[21] Strategic intervention by the fourth generation of leaders, headed by Richard Eu, ex-CEO and current chairman of Eu Yan Sang, changed this bleak trajectory of the firm's development.[22] By 1996, Eu Yan Sang's businesses in Hong Kong, Malaysia and Singapore were consolidated into one entity, with common shareholders and management.[23] In 2016, Eu Yan Sang was privatised and delisted from trading. Richard Eu explains: "As a family, you're under pressure to maintain this long-term shareholding. But with every generation, more beneficiaries come into being, so it is fragmented from generation to generation."[24] According to him, finding a long-term institutional shareholder will be a more favourable arrangement as it will provide more stability for the company's future development.

The Eu Yan Sang story may not be applicable in other contexts, yet it does illustrate, in a sobering way, the possible perils of dispersed ownership. When ownership becomes too fragmented, there tends to be less incentive for shareholders to do the heavy lifting, to think and act long-term. More ominously, when owners do not have a stewardship mindset, they can behave like agents, not stewards, which threatens to destabilise the development and jeopardise the survival of a company, as seen from the unexpected mass disposal of Eu Yan Sang shares by the family members in Hong Kong. There are also positive examples of stewardship that we can draw from the narrative. The professionals who consolidated Eu Yan Sang's disparate business operations across different geographical locations were stewards with an ownership mentality. They acted in the best interests of owners and tackled challenging issues.

While Eu Yan Sang is a family business, the challenges it faces apply equally to companies owned by the state, institutions, or thousands of dispersed shareholders. At times, a discussion on the concept of ownership gets easily side-tracked by a debate on the merits or setbacks of different types of ownership structures. Long-lived, successful, well-stewarded companies have different ownership structures. However, what they have in common is the owners' and leaders' sense of responsibility to the company, and obligation to the people they serve. They are committed to the company's purpose and values initiated by their founders and perpetuated beyond a single generation. If leaders show by their actions that they are prepared to put the success of the enterprise ahead of their personal advantage, other people will follow. That is the way to create an ownership mentality. The ownership mentality is the edge that stewardship capitalism has over extractive capitalism. A company cannot thrive and sustain itself unless the nexus between ownership and stewardship is understood, that those who are entrusted with assets or wealth of any kind have an obligation to hand those assets on in a better shape than when they received them. The obligation to be a good steward applies to everyone in the entire wealth-creation value chain: investors, entrepreneurs, shareholders, asset managers as well as directors, managers and employees.

	O
Well-stewarded companies instil and nurture an ownership mentality. Owners and employees take responsibility and action as well as develop a sense of collective pride to forge proactive and integrative solutions to complex problems and dynamic situations. They see the organisation as an extension of themselves and act wholeheartedly with the interest of the company in mind. They engage and galvanise the diverse parts of the organisation towards a common goal with a collective sense of success and failure. Through a culture that emphasises personal as well as collective accountability, employees are clear about their individual roles as well as shared responsibilities. Taking ownership over time translates in action into: taking responsibility, taking care and taking pride. (Adapted from Stewardship Asia Centre's *Stewardship Principles for Family Businesses*)	W N E R S H I P

Box 2: Ownership

Purpose

Foremost among the reasons for the success of lasting companies is a clear sense of purpose guided by strong values. Having a clear purpose and values serves two functions: Firstly, these trigger aspirations and motivate all in the company; and secondly, they give a sense of direction when translating intent into mission for action. Well-stewarded companies succeed in crystallising and transmitting their founders' values and thoughts through precepts and codes of conduct. This institutionalised sense of purpose and core values help guide them through good and bad times.

Leaders cannot inspire people to do an outstanding job without clear purpose and a confidence that this is a purpose worth committing to. As economies mature, people are less often driven to work by the need for survival, and money alone cannot buy excellence. What motivates people to be committed and effective is the sense that what they are doing is important and meaningful, that those with whom they work value them, and what they are doing is of value to others. That is what the best companies, those with a sense of purpose, are able to draw from their people. And when it comes to the purpose itself, it goes beyond profit. Former P&G marketing director Jim Stengel conducted a ten-year study of 50,000 brands around the world. The conclusions surprised him. What emerged from his research was "the business value of ideals". The study concluded that companies which put people's lives at the centre of what they do usually outperformed the market by a large margin. In the case of the fifty most successful brands, they had chosen to connect with "one of the five fields of fundamental human values: eliciting joy, enabling connection, inspiring exploration, evoking pride and impacting society".[25]

Economist John Kay has described the negative consequences when listed companies abandon a statement of human purposes, keeping nothing more than a statement about shareholder value. As an illustration, he compared two mission statements from Imperial Chemical Industries (ICI), one from the 1980s and one from the 1990s. The first statement was expressed in terms of the needs of customers, employees and communities, as well as shareholders. The second put shareholders and the financial dimension first. Ironically, shareholder value was destroyed once the company put shareholders first.[26] "Maximising shareholder wealth" or "profit maximisation" were fashionable objectives in the 1990s but, as the evidence that is summarised in this and the next chapter will demonstrate, this preoccupation is rarely to be found in the statement of purpose of companies that have been successful for the long haul. As one recent summary of the evidence on corporate longevity put it:

> Among other common characteristics, these studies suggest that if companies are to inspire their own people, their customers and other stakeholders with loyalty and achieve high levels of commitment, the purpose has to be one to which human beings can relate beyond simply making money for themselves or their owners. This is not instead of making money. It is as well as making money. Many companies who focus on purpose beyond profit clearly state their purpose in a 'both/and' way.[27]

Increasingly, a company's articulated purpose is also seen as important to the various stakeholders. Employees ask why they would get themselves fully engaged in a company that says its purpose is to create shareholder value. For any business whose competitive position depends on its brand and public trust, the articulated purpose has to reflect values to which people can relate. Investors, too, are beginning to ask companies about their purpose. In his 2019 Letter to CEOs,

Larry Fink, CEO of BlackRock, the world's largest investor, describes the volatile and difficult business landscape, and then says: "Every company needs a framework to navigate this difficult landscape, and that it must begin with a clear embodiment of your company's purpose in your business model and corporate strategy."

Patagonia is a case where clearly-defined purpose and values steered a company to success in terms of its profitability for the company, the environment as well as the community it serves. Founded in 1973, Patagonia started off making tools for climbing. It has since grown to sell quality sportswear for a variety of sports, as well as hard-wearing clothes for outdoor labour.

Being firm in its purpose, Patagonia recognised from the start that saving the environment is in the long-term interests of all. The company's core mission or purpose states that Patagonia aims to use its resources, its business, its investments, its voice and its imagination to stop climate change.[28] Commendable for its clearly defined purpose and value system, the company is also unique in recognising the need to not only address the symptoms of global warming such as environmental degradation but also the causes. It acknowledges that business is still more part of problem than the solution and aims to "not only to do less harm, but to do more good".[29]

Patagonia achieves its aim of lowering environmental impact in a number of ways. Firstly, the company practises sustainability by ensuring that the clothes it makes are durable, and by providing clothing-repair services such that they rarely need to be replaced. It even puts out advertisements encouraging customers not to buy new outerwear and instead repair or, at the very least, give away or pass down their clothes through the generations.[30] It also strives to use recycled materials such as polyester, nylon, wool and down so as to lower environmental impact. Secondly, Patagonia donates "at least

1 per cent" of its sales profit to environmentally-focused grassroots organisations worldwide so it can help protect the planet and "protect what's irreplaceable".[31] Patagonia's founder Yvon Chouinard, together with another entrepreneur Craig Mathews, founder of Blue Ribbon Flies, started *One Percent for The Planet*, a group of businesses, non-profits and individuals who work together to fight climate change.[32]

Thirdly, Patagonia's textiles are bluesign certified, which means that the company uses sustainable methods to produce textiles by "eliminating harmful substances at each step of the supply chain, and approving chemicals, processes, materials and products that are safe for the environment, workers and customers".[33] This way, the company also takes care of its employees and customers by ensuring their health and safety.

Another benefit of having such a defined purpose is that the company acknowledges the innovation and agility needed to respond to the challenges that enable it to keep its mandate of protecting the environment. An example is how Patagonia responded to accusations by animal rights group Four Paws of abusing the geese from which it gets its down for its best-selling down jackets.[34] Patagonia found out that its suppliers were sourcing down from birds which were force-fed for meat and live-plucked up to four times during their life cycle. Live-plucking is the practice where the down feathers are plucked from a living goose while holding the bird immobile. It is a painful process where the birds are in intense pain and are often wounded. Patagonia responded to the accusation by working with animal welfare experts and also an independent third-party traceability specialist to "ensure each link in its supply chain was independently audited to meet best practices in animal welfare". It also helped set up the Global Traceable Down Standard which "guarantees that the birds are not force-fed or live-plucked".[35]

Patagonia is an example of how well-stewarded businesses can work to protect the planet, care for their stakeholders — including both their employees and customers — while still making a profit.

Well-stewarded companies are clear on the purpose of their existence. Their business decisions and operations are driven by a strong commitment to purpose, anchored on their values. These values, which are built, strengthened and passed down over time, are the fundamentals that act like compass bearings for the companies in action. In practice, they help to articulate and communicate clearly the purpose of the business and responsible wealth creation. This can be transmitted through their charter, constitution, philosophy, vision, mission statement and even shared stories. The companies live out the organisational purpose and values consistently such that they are embedded in their communication, actions and thinking processes. They are built upon a value-alignment process, on an ongoing basis, for both existing and new stakeholders. This ensures that the transcendental purpose and values will be continually imbibed and imparted as the company grows. (Adapted from Stewardship Asia Centre's *Stewardship Principles for Family Businesses*)	**P** **U** **R** **P** **O** **S** **E**

Box 3: Purpose

Relationships

Across a variety of businesses, there is one generalisation that can be made: every company has a number of significant relationships. Every company will stand or fall, depending on its ability to create value, establish stability and earn trust and loyalty in those relationships. Business success is driven by the health of the company's relationships with five key stakeholders — customers, employees, suppliers, shareholders and the community. The strength of the relationships is determined by the leadership's ability to align the relationships in loyalty and commitment to their purpose, like a magnet exercising its force until all the iron filings point in the same direction. Each company has to work out for itself what it has to do to succeed, and this means taking the trouble to understand the needs of each stakeholder and then meeting these needs in a balanced way. For a business to survive and thrive amid the inevitable shocks and changes that it will face, and for it to ride the wave of opportunities that accompany them, it needs to strengthen and secure its business model by building strong relationships based on trust, mutual benefit and reciprocity.

Businesses compete in the market, and they live or die by the quality of their relationships. It is in relationships with stakeholders that value is created. It is through relationships that a business learns and innovates. If those relationships are to be successful, the companies need the people who represent them, especially their employees or joint-venture partners, to think, speak and act as if they own the business. To achieve this level of instinctive alignment of stakeholders with the purpose of the business, leaders have to foster a spirit of ownership.

A catering and event planning company based in Elk Grove Village, Illinois, US, Tasty Catering is an example of a company that deeply engages with one of its key sets of stakeholders — its employees — and focuses on relationship-building with them beyond a rights-based approach. The company has put in place processes that actively encourage its employees to take ownership of their work, make decisions based on core values and innovate to build up the company. It does this by practising the following five approaches.

The first approach involves "support[ing] team members' freedom and responsibility".[36] The company trusts its employees to do what is needed without micromanaging them. This high level of trust enables the company to build solid relationships as reciprocity between the management and workers is heightened. With a high level of trust, Tasty Catering also gives its employees the freedom to innovate within the boundaries of their job in order to improve processes.

The second approach which the company practised was a change in mindset, especially by the management. Tasty Catering's CEO Tom Walter said he found it a challenge to switch from a more top-down "command and control" mindset to one where his employees are given the freedom to carry out their responsibilities. It became easier to make the switch once he realised that a controlling mindset was limiting the company to only the CEO's capabilities instead of making use of everyone's combined knowledge and capabilities.

Thirdly, the company encourages its employees to embrace its core values and to make decisions based on those values. This leads to positive behavioural norms and encourages employees to keep one another in line when undesirable behaviour arises.

The fourth approach is positive reinforcement. The company rewards and encourages those who practise their core values. This builds trust between management and workers as there is recognition and praise when one is seen to be practising those values.

Lastly, Tasty Catering demonstrates its support for entrepreneurial thinking by its employees by ensuring that they have the tools and resources to take action. Employees who have business ideas are encouraged and financially supported. If they succeed, these employees are often made the CEOs of their own satellite companies.[37] For example, since joining Tasty Catering in 2006, logistics manager Jamie Pritscher has started two new businesses financed and supported by Tasty Catering — a gift-basket company, of which she is the CEO, and a marketing firm.[38] Businesses started by employees often support Tasty Catering's operations in some way and take the role of other types of stakeholders, such as suppliers, and work to enhance their overall financial performance. Tasty Catering also makes its financial information transparent to its employees so everyone knows the profit margin. This encourages them to focus on "generating sales, cutting expenses, and looking for alternative sources of revenue", effectively building their entrepreneurial spirit and ownership mentality.

This approach has met with resounding success and gained the firm numerous accolades, including Forbes' America's Best Small Companies Award, the APA National Award for Psychologically Healthiest Workplace and the 101 Best and Brightest Workplace National Award. It has also been named *Wall Street Journal*'s Best Small Workplace and *Catering Magazine*'s National Caterer of the Year. This relationship-building also enabled Tasty Catering to retain its human capital. Its employee turnover is "less than 2% in an industry where 50% is the norm".[39] Therefore, a workplace with a good relationship-building culture inspires loyalty among its employees and creates value for mutual benefit.

Well-stewarded companies believe that stable and strong relationships with and among various stakeholders need to be established and carefully maintained. They leverage such established relationships to resolve conflicts. They cultivate an organisational culture that promotes open communication and tolerance, where employees can share ideas and resolve differences in a consensual manner via conflict-resolution mechanisms. They develop long-standing relationships with internal and external stakeholders. They promote reciprocal trust, kindness and compassion, and foster win-win collaboration with partners. (Adapted from Stewardship Asia Centre's *Stewardship Principles for Family Businesses*)	R E L A T I O N S H I P S

Box 4: Relationships

Long-term view

Business leaders embrace stewardship when they take on a long-term perspective. When asked how one could reconcile the short-term pressures that a company faces with its desire to be run for the long term, CEO of Temasek Holdings, Ho Ching, elaborated on the importance of acting today with tomorrow in mind:

> We do recognise that you cannot be there for the long term if you don't take care of your short term. One cannot have 30 bowls of rice 30 years from now, and zero bowls for the next 30 days. So there has to be a balance between the short-term and the longer-term deliverables. But if we over-focus on the short-term deliverables, we may run the risk of doing that at the expense of [the] long term.[40]

Stewardship in a disruptive world is about being able to balance the long term and also keep an eye on the short term. Paying attention to the long term while neglecting the short term is poor stewardship. So is acting today with no concern for tomorrow. It is not going to get the company beyond its day-to-day survival, and it is clear suicide for the long term. Stewardship motivates us to care for our responsibilities in such a way that over time, we hand over what we have inherited in better shape than before. Stewardship links past and present to the future. It involves "keeping an eye on your telescope for ... the long-term ... changes that will disrupt your industry, and keeping your other eye on the microscope, where you have to look after your stakeholders and your stakeholders' short-term needs".[41]

Often the debate on short-term and long-term perspectives gets embroiled in what constitutes the appropriate time horizon. Some fund managers say that they do not talk about long or short term, but the "right term". What time horizon then constitutes the "right term"? The debate is really about accountability, taking responsibility for your action or inaction. It is irresponsible to act either for the long or short term, knowing that you would not be answering for the consequence of that action or inaction.

Alibaba, a China-based online retail giant, is an example of a company where long-term thinking has led to success. As an eminent disruptor in the retail ecosystem with a forward-looking stance, it has helped many small businesses reach out to the world and improved consumers' retail experience at an unprecedented scale. Since its inception in 1999, Alibaba has been experiencing exponential growth, so much so that it became the second Asian company to break the US$500 billion valuation mark in 2018.[42]

Long-term thinking seems to be the basis of many of the business decisions made at Alibaba. On its website, the company states that it aims to "build the future infrastructure of commerce" and sees itself lasting for at least 102 years. This suggests that Alibaba is clear about its intent to be around for the long haul. With that vision, it will have to undertake a different path from businesses that are just gunning for quick flips and early exits. Such long-term outlook sets the value orientation of the company, as exemplified by its founder, Jack Ma. He has said: "Our challenge is to help more people make healthy money, 'sustainable money', money that is not only good for themselves but also good for the society."[43]

Integral to Alibaba's long-term vision to meet changing customer needs is its ability to harness market feedback loops. Based on market intelligence, Alibaba has established a notable retail ecosystem over the years. Starting from a simple aim to connect buyers with sellers, its retail infrastructure has ballooned to integrate innovations such as merchant rating, social interaction, and secured payment, to enhance the procurement experience.[44] From the outset, these seem to be merely changes in architecture, but in reality, these changes have removed obstacles to online transactions, thereby propelling radical and lasting changes to production and consumption culture.

In Ma's letter to shareholders, the founder reiterated Alibaba's long-term goal. He wrote:

> In 20 years, we hope to serve 2 billion consumers around the world, empower 10 million profitable businesses and create 100 million jobs. This will be an even more difficult journey than the one behind us.[45]

Alibaba aims to venture into global markets and use cloud computing to support markets. This has presented challenges. While Alibaba has fulfilled its purpose of making it easy to do business anywhere, its platform has unwittingly become a nefarious haven for the sale of counterfeit products.[46] Recognising that counterfeiting can undermine its long-term growth, and in a broader sense, the country's growth as a responsible economic power, the company stepped up its efforts to collaborate with international bodies to combat the issue.[47] Such commitment to think long term and not to succumb to short-term gains is perhaps one of the best defence mechanisms that a company such as Alibaba can have when addressing the onslaught of precarious threats in a disruptive age.

Well-stewarded companies do not neglect long-term considerations in the face of pressure from increasing short-termism. They adopt a long-term orientation towards spending and investment, favouring sustainable growth over quick gains. They ensure that short-term decisions are in line with long-term goals. They contemplate the long-term consequences of actions. They leverage their long-standing competitive advantages so that they can continue the long-term development of the business. They look beyond short-term profitability and temporary gains. They focus on the preservation of intangible values for long-term success and legacy-building.

(Adapted from Stewardship Asia Centre's *Stewardship Principles for Family Businesses*)

L O N G I T E R M   V I E W

Box 5: Long-term View

Community

Companies need to invest, not just in areas that are beneficial to themselves, but also in other areas that will benefit the community at large. As aggregators of wealth, resources and talent, with local and potentially global outreach, companies have a responsibility to create products and services that are of value to society. They provide platforms for partnerships and play a role in community building that cannot be duplicated. Companies have a role in nation-building as well, especially in developing countries. An example is Ayala Corporation in the Philippines. Its role in the country's economic development is one of the key reasons for its success.

Mere lip service in terms of CSR activities cannot be counted as community contribution anymore. Companies need to be aware that their key stakeholders — investors, consumers, business partners, and the global community at large — are increasingly conscious of values and sustainability. They want to partner, work for, buy from and interact with good companies. In the long term, this will be the most important factor for a company's survival, and it is inextricable from stewardship.

Banyan Tree, a Singapore-based company, understands this well, and puts it across not in mere statement but in action. Established in 1994, Banyan Tree Holdings is an international hospitality brand that operates across Asia, America, Africa and the Middle East. The company's first hotel was built on a derelict mining site in Phuket that was originally declared by the United Nations Development Program Planning unit and the Tourism Authority of Thailand to be unfit for ecological restoration. After an extensive rehabilitation effort, the rejuvenated site, now known as Laguna Phuket, has put its grim beginnings behind.[48] With the successful remediation of toxic land came buoyant economic revitalisation and meaningful community uplifting for the region.

Claire Chiang, chairperson for the Banyan Tree Global Foundation, said:

> Enabling long term societal prosperity for communities is central to Banyan Tree's ability to create value for stakeholders. Our resorts have implemented numerous site and region specific initiatives addressing community empowerment issues identified by host communities.[49]

With the firm belief that businesses and their stakeholders can partake in value co-creation, the company encourages both the local community and the hotel's patrons to become change-makers for social and economic advancement. Through the Banyan Tree Gallery initiative, local artisans are helped to sustain their livelihoods by the promotion of fair labour practices, indigenous culture, craft development, mentorship of business acumen and access to international distribution networks. Plugging into the local community, the company engages local schools to provide equipment and infrastructure to create a conducive learning environment. Additionally, the Laguna Phuket Kindergarten, which is regarded as one of the best in Thailand, has been set up to provide free childcare services for children of community members and associates. When calamities strike, Banyan Tree works with local authorities, mobilises its workforce and sets up disaster-recovery funds to provide humanitarian aid, building social resilience in the host countries.[50]

Besides social empowerment, Banyan Tree also shows steadfast commitment towards the cause of environmental conservation. To safeguard the environment, Banyan Tree collaborates with policymakers, NGOs, academics, biologists and universities worldwide to support environmental research, conservation, restoration and awareness-raising initiatives.[51] Such efforts have culminated in concrete action for coral restoration, as well as the development of toolkits for monitoring sustainability and conservation efforts. The company considers financial, social and environmental implications at every stage of its business operations. With these careful deliberations, many stakeholders have benefited from Banyan Tree's stewardship: the local people who have become agents of change themselves, researchers whose findings have contributed to the knowledge base of their scientific community, as well as hotel patrons who have benefited from a thriving community. At Banyan Tree Holdings, stewardship is not just rhetoric, but a tapestry of synergistic efforts leading to a profound transformation of communities.

As they grow, well-stewarded companies adopt a broader definition of success to include doing well, doing good and doing right. They see businesses as an integral part of society. They extend their reach to the wider community. They establish a presence in the community, share the wider benefits of their operations, work with the community and communicate with it — bearing in mind that the trust of the public is an important factor in driving business growth and innovation. They strive to create positive economic, social and environmental impact. By giving back to society, non-economic wealth such as social capital, communal ties, reputation and core values will be preserved and passed on. They integrate social responsibility into their corporate philosophy, identifying the social causes that resonate with them and where they can create impact — these commitments should be embedded as mainstream and not piecemeal business activities. Social responsibility is not to be seen as a separate part of the business operation, but part of the overall stewardship mindset of the business.

(Adapted from Stewardship Asia Centre's *Stewardship Principles for Family Businesses*)

C O M M U N I T Y

Box 6: Community

Chapter 3

Steward Leadership and the Pursuit of Long-term Success

In Chapter 1, we described the stewardship mindset as being based on inclusive, as opposed to exclusive, thinking about the nature of business. In Chapter 2, we defined stewardship as the responsible and wholehearted management of inherited assets, so as to pass them on in a better condition. We explained that stewardship starts with the will, with the determination to achieve and deliver in a unique way, and not to wait for others to dictate the path. It connects the past and present with the future, and it flows from a sense of interdependence. We articulated and illustrated the five core concepts of stewardship in thinking and practice — ownership, purpose, long-term view, relationships and community. In this chapter, we look at what the stewardship mindset means for leaders, and how steward leaders define, pursue and share success in ways that make sense for employees, shareholders and society.

The decision that a leader makes to lead in the spirit of stewardship rarely stems from a cold analysis of the evidence. Stewardship grows out of one's belief and character. Great steward leaders display the courage of their convictions.

There is, nonetheless, an impressive body of research evidence from Asia, Europe and the US that connects the elements and concepts of stewardship with enduring and successful companies. Professor Funabashi's research on Japan, described in the previous chapter, concluded that the key to long company life was leadership driven by clear values, which no doubt has significant influence on the other principles cited, including — vision and mission, a strong sense of legacy, a vision of the long-term, an emphasis on the value of people, a commitment to society, nation-building, customer orientation, innovation, and continuous improvement.

Professors Jim Collins and Jerry Porras conducted a study of America-based companies which outperformed the US stock market by fifteen times over fifty years.[1] After a paired comparison exercise with similar companies that performed significantly worse, they observed that the high-performing companies tend to view leadership as transcending the qualities of any one individual, that they tend to have an enduring core purpose beyond just making money, and that they had achieved strong consistency between stated and actual values.

The former Shell head of planning, Arie de Geus, conducted a study for his CEO about the common features of long-lived companies which were older than Shell.[2] He found that what they had in common were conservatism in financing, sensitivity to the environment, a sense of cohesion and identity in their employees, and an ability to delegate and show "tolerance at the margin". All these reinforce the findings from Jim Stengel, Stewardship Asia Centre and Tomorrow's Company, cited in the previous chapter.

There is, then, a solid foundation for the belief that financial prudence, an ownership mentality, inspiring purpose, clear values, as well as deep and effective relationships which reach out to the needs of community and society are the evidence-based approaches that are logical for any leaders focused on success, now and in the long term.

Take any enduring and successful business, and you will find a strong sense of what the company is for, and what it stands for through successive generations. The other generalisation you can make, across all industry sectors, is about the strength and health of a company's relationships with its customers, employees, suppliers, community and shareholders. The health of these relationships form the company's antennae. They serve as an early warning system for market shifts to come and allow the company to learn from past inefficiences. Operational and transactional efficiency is a necessary condition for the immediate survival of a business.

STEWARD LEADERSHIP: A VIRTUOUS CIRCLE OF LEADERSHIP AND GOVERNANCE

Steward leaders develop their own dynamic way of doing and thinking about business. They lead with impact, safeguard the future and drive social good.[3] They start with a purpose, describing whom the business exists to serve and what it aspires to achieve. They identify the key relationships that contribute to success. They set out clearly what the company stands for, and how it expects to behave in all its relationships, including vital ones with the community and society with which the business is so interdependent. Steward leaders inspire and enable people involved in those key relationships to understand and commit themselves to the goals and values of the organisation. There will be a constant balancing of the *what* and the *how*, the performance and the behaviours, the hard and the soft. This balancing is a vital ingredient for longer-term success. It is crucial for trust, reputation, risk management and the development of the real and metaphorical *licence to operate*. It flows through the whole approach to success, including the definition of the business model and the clarification of the time horizon to which the business is working. In later chapters, when discussing the role of the board and investors, the terms *value* and *mandate* become central. The same is true for the executives leading an organisation. They ensure that everyone knows what success looks like. They communicate the nature of the value they are creating, and for whom. While setting the objective, they are defining a mandate which governs both what their people will strive to achieve, and how they will act. It is the board's job to satisfy itself that this task is undertaken and regularly renewed.

It is always tempting for a newly appointed leaders to emphasise the ways in which they are different from their predecessors. Yet, the effectiveness of an organisation's purpose, values and relationships depends on continuity. The best CEOs are what Professors Collins and Porras described as "clock builders, not time-tellers".[4] They acknowledge what they inherited from their predecessors and leave behind a legacy of behaviours that endure beyond them.[5] While a focus on succession is vital, organisations will not always have the best CEOs. Individual leaders come and go. As we will show in the later chapters, companies need the combined stewardship contribution of their boards, owners and employees to ensure that certain important things stay constant even as the organisation changes and, from time to time, loses its way.

Every individual leader will have her or his own style. Yet, wherever one can observe a well-led organisation with an enduring record of success, one will also find some common steps that leaders would have taken to embed stewardship in the organisation.

Steward leaders have a joined-up way of thinking about success. This is best described as a virtuous circle of leadership and governance which integrates all the activities of leaders and managers into a coherent whole. It is a circle in which each stage gives meaning to the next. At its centre lies the organisation's purpose and values. The circle links business planning, measurement, production, reporting and dialogue with shareholders and stakeholders. This integrated approach is a defence against the compartmentalised thinking that too often handicaps organisations and prevents them from reaching their potential. It prompts managers to consider the under-developed potential of each relationship and to achieve success through relationships integral to the business model. It focuses the mind on how to achieve high levels of engagement, trust and loyalty in all its relationships. It links the business model to the purpose, and the reward and recognition systems of the company to both. It offers a balanced basis for the measurement and reporting of all the factors that are relevant to the achievement of the business purpose, including its wider impact on the community and its commitment to the longer term.

None of these stages in the virtuous circle of leadership and governance take place in isolation. The selection of key performance indicators flows from the business model. The business model builds on the purpose and the values, and describes the part each

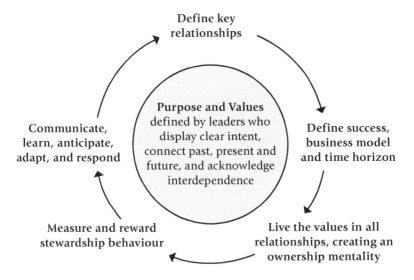

Figure 1: Virtuous Circle of Leadership and Governance

relationship may have in contributing to enduring success, and the part that behaviour across the business will play in achieving success. A company's approach to the thorny issue of pay and rewards flows from this balanced understanding of what success looks like. It reflects the combined importance of hitting financial targets and behaving in the right way while pursuing them. Reporting on performance not only provides verification of whether or not the company has achieved what it sets out to do, but also helps start a conversation about progress in different relationships to reach the intended goal. An effective process of reporting and dialogue should be a learning experience for all participants, especially for the leaders of the organisation, about the current levels of trust in, and loyalty to, the company in all its key relationships.

SETTING OUT PURPOSE AND VALUES

Clear purpose and strong values will be evident in any well-stewarded company, as we saw in Chapter 2. We feel most alive when we are involved in projects bigger than ourselves. That is what the best companies inspire in their people. The evidence is that people are so much more energised by a purpose which goes beyond their own self-interest.[6] This applies in different ways to people who are clients, customers and consumers. As the study by Jim Stengel that was quoted in the previous chapter shows, a commitment to the human purposes of business is vital for underpinning loyalty, reputation, trust and the company's brand — all the factors which are known to drive profitability in the long term. Steward leaders recognise the need to connect with the human perspectives of business. That is why they start with purpose and values. They communicate their sense of purpose and vision for the organisation in ways that engage people. They then seek to create a shared understanding of and commitment to the business objectives and the business model. They bring purpose and values alive in all the relationships of the business.

As we argued in Chapter 2, enduring and successful companies have a purpose that goes beyond profit. Steward leaders lead with impact by motivating and engaging employees through enhanced awareness and acceptance of the group's purpose and mission, and by inspiring them to look beyond their own self-interest for the collective good. Peter Senge's "purpose story" illustrates this compelling need for purpose.[7] He describes how a transcendental narrative that connects at both the personal and universal levels can act as a galvanising force. It can serve as a common mental model to inspire people to contribute with passion and to empower everyone to create lasting value. There is the need to align values and actions, and the tone for this is set from the top. Steward leaders will lead by example. They will awaken and strengthen the organisational conscience of their businesses and accentuate these values in a manner that is easily accepted by colleagues and stakeholders of the business. These values serve as a linchpin across decisions, without which it would be difficult to achieve consistency of action.

Defining Key Relationships

Businesses compete in the market to serve human purposes. Leaders align relationships to the company's purpose and values in order to create enduring success. The authors John Kotter and James Heskett found that companies with strong relationships with key stakeholder constituencies were more successful because they were better able to adapt.

Firms with cultures that emphasised all the key managerial constituencies (customers, stockholders and employees) and leadership from managers at all levels outperformed firms that did not have these cultural traits by a huge margin. Over an eleven-year period, the former increased revenues by an average of 682% v. 166% for the latter, expanded their workforces by 282% v 36%, grew their stock prices by 901% v. 74%, and improved their net incomes by 756% v 1%.[8]

In the United States, Eric Ryan and Adam Lowry, founders of Method, have transformed the cleaning industry by understanding their customers' needs. Method, which is now owned by SC Johnson, is a company that sells green cleaning products.[9] The concept had its genesis in the duo's strong aversion to using cleaning products that contained toxic ingredients. At that time, the only available "eco-conscious" alternatives were ineffective. They realised from their own experience that consumers wanted something better, and so they founded Method with the aim of catalysing a revolution which they dubbed "people against dirty".[10] They understood that consumers wanted products that were not only less environmentally damaging, but also aesthetically pleasing, such that they could be displayed in the open. This paved the way for the sleek design of Method's products. In their book, the co-founders attributed their success to the strategy of fostering deeper relationships with fewer customers within a niche green market. In other words, they have identified and learnt from their key relationships. They emphasised that everything they knew, they learnt from the millions of customers who engaged with their brand daily.[11] In fact, their customers are their best advocates. Through the customer feedback channel, customers propagated the benefits of their products in a manner akin to that of evangelistic fervour.[12]

Chetna Gala Sinha, the founder and chair of India's Mahila Sahakari Bank and Mann Deshi Foundation, is a leader who has placed relationships at the centre of her business. Working close to the ground, she understands the plight of rural women who have limited access to financial support and this inspired her to uplift the community. She decided to help link them to the market. Sinha's first breakthrough came when she started the country's first bank for and by rural women in Maharashtra.[13] The provision of microfinancing and the introduction of financial literacy programmes have lifted many women out of abject poverty by giving them the know-how to participate in fruitful economic activities.

Additionally, living up to her mantra of "never provide poor solutions to poor people",[14] she introduced many timely improvisations to the banking system, notably, the birth of doorstep banking.[15] These incremental efforts have helped budding female entrepreneurs build financial security. Sinha's bank has so far helped over 310,000 women, of whom 84,000 took loans to become entrepreneurs in their own right. The bank's working capital has grown from over US$10,300 in 1997 to US$21,852,000 in 2017.[16] Sinha leads with impact through understanding and acting on ground sentiment, safeguards the future through well-conceived plans, and drives social good through empowering the less privileged.

The Community

To steward leaders, the community or wider society is not just another stakeholder. Both provide the ground from which the enterprise was grown in the first place.

A prime example of a steward leader whose company is committed to improving the quality of life in the communities it serves is Vineet Rai, the founder of Aavishkaar-Intellecap Group, a social venture capital firm. He focuses particularly on making investments in distressed and difficult areas where the "ecosystem is under-developed or even non-existent".[17] Milk Mantra, a start-up that focuses on agricultural dairy products, is one of the company's investments. Srikumar Misra, the founder of Milk Mantra, pointed out that the organised distribution of milk in the eastern Indian state of Odisha was less than half of that of the rest of India. He wanted to improve the situation. Recognising the need to bring capital to underserved localities, Aavishkaar poured in US$700,000 to support the entrepreneur.[18] The business has since scaled exponentially. By 2017, Milk Mantra had built an entire supply chain, successfully sourcing its supply from 46,000 smallholder farmers across 400 collection centres located in local villages — an increase of almost eightfold from a modest start of 6,000 farmers in its network.[19] Today, Milk Mantra provides jobs for thousands and brings in a revenue of over US$21 million.[20] By venturing into a territory where no previous resources existed, Rai has truly empowered the poor by creating opportunities. In addition, by engaging deeply with companies, Rai nurtures new ventures to create successful and sustainable business models which spin off to become credible business and community resources.

Steward leaders see businesses as an integral part of society. They strive to create positive economic, social and environmental impact. They keep track of external and internal stakeholders' expectations for the company. They build solid relationships, and ensure that there is a positive two-way exchange between corporations and their broader societal context. They drive social good at multiple levels. In the broadest sense, steward leaders are globally conscious and care deeply about the welfare of the global community. At the micro level, steward leaders care about the well-being of individuals and their neighbourhoods. They show an understanding of the interconnected world and a commitment on which the symbiotic development of relationships and businesses thrives.

Stakeholders

An emphasis on relationships is often described as "a stakeholder approach". There is a good reason to be careful about using the word "stakeholder" or confusing a steward leader's approach with "stakeholder theory".

This is because "Stakeholder" is one of those words that has become overused and risks becoming meaningless. There are four particular problems with the word. First, it is ambiguous. It is sometimes used to mean all those who have a relationship with the business, including shareholders. More often, as will be the case in this book, it is used to describe all non-shareholder relationships.

There is a second sort of ambiguity. Very often, the term is used to describe people on whom the business has an impact. But this is to ignore the most important question — who are the people who will make the biggest contribution to the success of the business? Relationships are key to the success of any business, and it is *reciprocity* that is the key to enduring relationships. It is impossible to identify how the business will create value unless you start by having a clear picture of the customers, employees and suppliers who will make that success possible. Any "stakeholder analysis" which limits itself to those stakeholders upon whom the business will have an impact, is steering the business away from the key contributors of its success.

The third problem with the term "stakeholder" is closely linked to the second. Not only does it tend to ignore the issue of people's contribution to success, it is also often used in an undifferentiated way. The term does not communicate much if it extends from those who have a vital and continuing relationship with the company to those who may occasionally use the road outside its premises.

The fourth problem with the term "stakeholder" was touched on in Chapter 1, in the discussion of three views of the company. Those who espouse a stakeholder view of the company tend to use phrases like "stakeholder democracy" or "stakeholder accountability". Advocates of stakeholder theory often fail to distinguish between the formal legal position and the informal one. It is important to start by acknowledging the former. In most jurisdictions, the directors of the company are formally accountable to its shareholders. Under most legal systems in the East or the West, those shareholders conduct elections to put the board in place, and can remove them at the annual meeting. Those legal formalities have to be respected before one moves on to an equally important reality that exists beyond any legal obligation: a company needs to behave as if it were accountable to other key groups who can influence its success, and upon whom it has an influence.

The company is a living organism. It creates value through the success of all its key relationships. The word "stakeholder" is an undifferentiated rights-focused way of talking about the company's relationships. (Perhaps it is more than coincidence that it includes within it the letters making up the word "take"!). Entrepreneurs and leaders start with contribution. For example, many discussions of employees as stakeholders concentrate on wages, benefits, working hours, holidays, time off — all the rights and entitlements of employees. But what about employees as contributors, producers, innovators, salespeople, measurers, monitors, protectors and ambassadors of the company? That is why steward leaders look beyond the mapping of stakeholders to the much more precise identification of key relationships through which value is created. This is a theme to which we return in Chapter 8, where we discuss the triple bottom line.

Defining Success, Business Model and Time Horizon

A stewardship approach towards business success is designed to create ever increasing value. Companies cannot create value for shareholders unless they are creating value in all their key relationships.

In defining success, and stating what they mean by value, steward leaders are putting together all the ingredients that will enable them to hand over the company in a better shape to their successors. Each company is different. Leaders have to work out what it has to do to succeed and what needs to be measured. This means taking the trouble to understand stakeholder needs in each key relationship, and then developing a business model meeting those needs in a way that is appropriate to the company's purpose and values. At the same time, this can form the basis of the way that the company measures and reports, under the principles of integrated reporting which are described below. This involves measuring and reporting on the company's deployment of all six capitals — financial capital, manufacturing capital, human capital, social and relationship capital, intellectual capital and natural capital.[21]

It also means finding the right balance between the requirements of the short, medium and long term. It involves asking what combination of people, place, organisation, price, technology, behaviour, reputation, market knowledge, and product or service design a company can deploy to create the value it desires.[22] In doing so, companies need to think, measure and then report in an integrated way. This involves two kinds of judgements — first, balancing the hard and the soft aspects of success, and second, seeing success as an integrated process and not as isolated activities.

"How does your company make money?" is a good question to ask in the boardroom. This may seem like an obvious question. It is surprising how different the answers can be around the table. However, it can be the starting point for a profound discussion within the organisation. Yet, there is also a broader question: what are all the ways in which your company aims to create value? This is the question which is implied by the logic of integrated reporting. To stimulate progress and innovation, good stewards throughout the system will insist that through integrated reporting, they receive relevant information about the company's deployment of all six capitals mentioned earlier.[23]

Thus, a business model is like a recipe. It describes how an organisation puts together all the ingredients that result, reliably and systematically, in a successful business outcome. The business model then informs the approach to measurement and reward. Many companies still suffer from a machine-age view of measurement. Their leaders assume that Key Performance Indicators (KPIs) and other numeric accounting information tell them all they need to know about success and failure. Sometimes, they even say "the numbers never lie" without stopping to ask who prepared those numbers, what assumptions they made and what incentives they might have which could influence their approach. Measurement needs to extend beyond the financial numbers to an understanding of the health of the employee, customer and supplier relationships, the perception of the company in the community and society, product quality, customer complaints, the rate of innovation and the feedback on how employees feel about the behaviour of their managers.

In their focus on safeguarding the future, steward leaders have to become "ambidextrous", combining short- and long-term perspectives in the development of their business model and in their approach to measurement and reporting.[24] They have to be prudent to secure survival through tough times, and yet also take calculated risks for growth. We, therefore, argue that:

> The importance of leadership thus extends into the future, and succession planning is possibly the most important stewardship responsibility. To meet the challenges of the future, today's leaders should not spare any effort to groom the next generation of successors who have the right values, traits and skills. If stewardship has been institutionalised in the organisation's culture through collective values, beliefs and practices, individuals who embody the notion of stewardship will naturally emerge and be candidates to become the future steward leaders.[25]

One might think that the time horizon would inevitably shorten in an age of volatility and rapid change. However, as was shown in the previous chapter, it turns out that the opposite is the case. An age of volatility must also be an age of agility. It takes time to create the conditions in which an organisation will be fast on its feet. This was well explained by Antony Jenkins, who has experience in both long-established business and young disruptors. Jenkins is the founder and executive chairman of 10x Future Technologies (a fintech company which he started in 2016) and the former CEO of Barclays:

> We're in a different era today, and the old days of strategic planning are over. The corporation that could be very 'planful' over the long term is a creature of the 20th century. We can't predict how technology is going to change our world, or what the next geopolitical hotspot will be. This ongoing volatility means companies must be agile. Yet you can't become agile overnight. Agility requires you to retool how an organisation operates and ask fundamental questions: What sort of people do we hire? How do we organise them? Does our culture appropriately support and reward risk-taking? Do we penalise failure, or regard it as a learning opportunity? While creating an agile business takes time, it is a key goal to pursue and fundamental to future success. Today's short term was yesterday's long term.[26]

One of the pitfalls for investors, analysts, non-executive directors and anyone trying to assess a business from the outside is that words can be impressive but they are not necessarily reflected in deeds. Too often, people look at purpose, values, KPIs, strategies, relationships or remuneration in isolation. The purpose may sound fine but is it compatible with the business model?

The 150-year-old Tata Group is an example of values dovetailing with the business model. For Jamsetji Tata, the founder, success was about enhancing the health of the society in which the company operated. He truly believed his company could and should be a force for good in society. This is what Sir Dorab Tata said about his father Jamsetji Tata:

> To my father, the acquisition of wealth was only a secondary object in life; it was always subordinate to the constant desire in his heart to improve the industrial and intellectual condition of the people of this country, and the various enterprises which he, from time to time, undertook in his lifetime had for their principal object the advancement of India in these important respects.[27]

Not every business will have such an ambitious statement of its place in the world. It does not need to. But what is important is that it translates into behaviour. The behaviour of Tata employees, even in crisis, reflects this. In accordance with company values, the Taj Hotel group, a Tata company, has developed a unique approach to recruiting staff directly from small towns, focusing more on hiring people with integrity and dedication than skills and talent. Additionally, the staff are trained for eighteen months rather than the average of twelve. The company believes in teaching people to improvise rather than doing things by the book and insisted that employees place guests' interests over the company's. A test of the Tata values came in November 2008, when terrorists entered the Taj Mahal Hotel in Mumbai, shooting and killing indiscriminately. After a night of terror, thirty-one people had died (of whom half were hotel staff) and twenty-eight were injured. Dozens of guests were saved by the calm and brave actions of the Taj's staff. Bhisham Mansukhani was a guest who escaped that night. Of the staff who saved his life when they could have run away, he said:

They were just kids. Young boys and girls. Two girls in their early 20s, couple of kitchen staff. Those brave girls had their phone on charging and were guiding the NSG [National Security Guard] to our location. They were remarkably great. One of them, Rajan Kamble, who was in front of us, was shot in the stomach while helping the guests escape. Over the period of 11 hours, the staff saved my life several times.[28]

LIVING THE VALUES IN ALL RELATIONSHIPS, CREATING AN OWNERSHIP MENTALITY

Linney is a Nottinghamshire-based family business founded in 1851. Until 1996, it was a newspaper publisher. Nick Linney became the CEO in 1980. He wanted to change the culture of the business which he felt was too "command & control". He initiated a profound process of change in the culture and business model.

The turnover of the residual printing business in 1996 was about USD 19 million. Twenty years later the approximate turnover of the group was USD 131 million and it had grown its workforce from 500 to nearly 1000. It now operates in high quality premises, employing state of the art equipment, and has diversified from printing into design, digital services, film production, broadcasting, social media, logistics and outsourced administration of all kinds, reflecting the "can do" values of the group.

Values lie at the core of the business and its success. These values underpin the strength of all the key relationships of the business. Nick, now chairs the holding company while his eldest son Miles is MD of the operating business. He runs a full day course on the core values of the business every month. This course is held for employees who have just joined the business and for those who last attended the course three years ago. Statements on values are also found everywhere on their site, and Linney group's six keywords are, "helpfulness, honesty, friendliness, co-operation, security, and prosperity".

What Nick Linney and his team have created is an ownership mentality across the entire workforce which permeates the company's approach to all its relationships. For over eight years now the daily production requirements have been delivered without shop floor managers, in self-managed teams, which have both shift and resource team leaders, sometimes on a rotating basis. Continuous Improvement Groups (CIGs) assist in longer term projects.

This is a good example of the power of company culture. It shows how values can be developed and shared effectively such that they result in behaviour with customers, suppliers and the community that generates competitive advantage and becomes essential to success.

Indeed, Linney himself says

> The real difference is culture: our culture is different from your culture…you instantly feel the culture in our family business.

The most successful companies may have manuals and clear policies — but they know they are relying on people's judgement in unforeseen, untested situations. The real test will come from challenges that no manual can anticipate. As the experience of Tata and the Taj Hotel Group shows, outstanding customer service cannot be learned by rote: people have to aspire to give that service and be equipped with a framework of trust and guidance that enables them to do so in their own way. The consumer businesses that are celebrated for exceptional service have instilled some general principles, and reinforced them by continual example, practice, and feedback. In the end, the success of these businesses is due to the right culture, values and leadership, and each outstandingly successful business finds a distinct and unique way of expressing these in practical ways that impress and convince its people.

MEASURING AND REWARDING STEWARDSHIP BEHAVIOURS

Like velcro, a useful everyday commodity that functions by bringing together two different surfaces, a successful business will combine two elements of different textures. The hard, gritty surface represents the nature of competition and cost management: winning in unforgiving markets, clarity, discipline and simplicity, rigorous measurement against the world's best, relentless cost focus, as well as restlessness, disruption and change. The other, the soft, pliable surface, represents the nature of collaboration and value-creation: self-expression, sensitivity to others and their mental and physical well-being and safety, being true to oneself, interdependence, creativity, openness, tolerance of diversity needed to encourage creativity, as well as loyalty.

If a business emphasises only the soft surface of success, then it will risk becoming too inward-looking. On the other hand, if it focuses solely on the hard surfaces and endlessly benchmarks itself against others, it will become an entity without flair or personality. To be enduring, a business must be able to recognise the importance of each surface, and the design of its success model will reflect a balance between the two. Its framework of measurement needs to reflect this balance. The framework of reporting also needs to follow through.

It is often said that what gets measured gets managed. This is true. It is also true that what gets measured gets manipulated, especially where there are incentives and bonuses riding on the results of the measurement.

Too often, leaders energetically introduce new KPIs without first defining the logic that should underpin them. All sorts of tools and techniques have been developed to help people with measurement. These tools can provoke thinking. They can be a useful framework for comparison and benchmarking. They can provide a common language for discussing what companies are trying to achieve. But measurement is not a virtue in itself. It only has meaning when viewed in the context of an organisation's purpose and business model. It is original thought that is needed if the intent is to devise a measurement and reporting framework which communicates the essence of the company.

Remuneration is another area where it is important to think about things in an integrated way, and this is covered in more detail in the next chapter on the role of the board. Many boards and investors are impressed by the idea of payment by results. But this is based on a misunderstanding of human motivation. As Daniel Pink put it:

> The best use of money as a motivator is to pay people enough to take the issue of money off the table. Pay people enough so they're not thinking about money and they're thinking about the work. Once you do that, it

turns out that there are three factors that science shows lead to better performance, not to mention personal satisfaction: autonomy, mastery and purpose.[29]

If results are defined without reference to the values of the business, disaster will likely follow, as it did in Enron. Why should employees of a company want to give their very best, if the company exists purely to make shareholders and top managers rich? The real clue to commitment and loyalty is found in the company's personality and character, and the feelings people have about it. This comes from the purpose and the values of the organisation, which in turn influence the way people are paid and treated. It is human nature to be willing to go further and be more committed to the company if you can see the importance of what it is doing and if your leaders have shown that they see you as important.

The best defence against major fraud or misjudgement is to have a clear set of values which people imbibe and follow. Steward leaders have to lead by example in rewarding adherence to those values and educating or penalising those who deviate from them. If everyone is aware of the values governing how business should be conducted, it is less likely that one rogue employee will go undetected even when the rules and formal controls break down. Someone, somewhere is likely to notice and mount a challenge or communicate their worries in a way that gets the attention of managers or senior management. If, on the other hand, everyone is made to feel that it is only results that count, people will hesitate before challenging the methods by which results are obtained. With an organisation-wide sense of purpose and values, to which all employees have a genuine commitment, every single employee could possibly help defend the organisation against potential wrongdoing. Just as the right culture in a factory is a stronger guarantor of health and safety than any list of *do's and don'ts*, however exhaustive they may be, a clear ethical tradition is the best guarantor against fraud and corporate disaster.

Reporting

The annual report is an important test of the company's determination to integrate the soft and the hard surfaces of success and create a coherent narrative. How many annual reports start with a clear statement from the CEO or Chairman in which they set out the company's purpose and values? How many companies' reports include a perspective about the extent to which employees in the business agree with the purpose and values? Too often, annual reports follow a predictable formula. The Public Relations (PR) department writes the warm words that appear under the chairman's name at the front. The finance department produces the financial figures at the back. While the financial results of all their efforts are factually recorded in the management and financial accounts, this does not always indicate success in a way that actually benefits the company or its stakeholders. The true story of a business is told only when the company describes where it has come from, why it exists, what it stands for, whom it serves, whom it employs and how it balances the demands from different stakeholders. This is integrated thinking. It can guide how leaders, the board and investors think about success. It is this logic that is now being reflected in the evolving practice of integrated reporting.

Wise company stewards will start with their own understanding of how their organisation achieves success and creates value. They will base their reporting on a measurement framework that reflects the ingredients for their company's success. To achieve this, they will insist on having a clear sense of the personality of the company as a whole. And this will lead boards, asset managers and asset owners to focus on clearly defining what is the value that the company or its portfolio of investments is aiming to create.

The growing focus on environmental sustainability and CSR risks making the situation worse. Too many companies now behave as though the world of CSR and sustainability is a parallel universe. The danger is that a separate department produces a separate set of numbers on carbon impact or philanthropic investments, in compliance with a set of guidelines, without contributing to a holistic story about the company's progress, achievements and impact. There are some CSR and Sustainability departments in companies which seem to regard the production of a sustainability report as an end in itself. But the best companies focus their communication on learning from their stakeholders. They assemble the numbers so that they can have an honest account of their company's progress. The real benefit comes from the dialogue that follows and the learning that comes with it.

COMMUNICATING, LEARNING, ANTICIPATING, ADAPTING AND RESPONDING

Organisations are increasingly evolving into networks and communities, often connected via the web. They cannot be treated as if they were giant pieces of machinery, where those "in charge" sit at the top, pressing buttons and pulling levers. The company is a living organism. Every cell in that organism has a life of its own, and with the help of social media, every cell can communicate with other cells inside and outside the organisation. Every cell affects and is affected by the world around it. In the face of an onslaught of different messages, what matters is the central nervous system, that is, the common impulses that stimulate and connect all the cells to achieve a common result. A company's reputation is therefore dependent on the quality of its relationships with its constituent "cells". This means that companies need the advocacy of stakeholders. Steward leaders need to spread the common purpose and values through every cell of the organism.

In their recent book, *New Power*, authors Henry Timms and Jeremy Heimans share this vision of the organisation as a living organism, not a machine. They describe the emergence of powerful new social networks. They contrast what they describe as New Power values with those of Old Power. Old Power can be found in the formalities of representative governance and professional expertise. New Power is characterised by informal networked governance, self-organisation, crowd wisdom, collaboration and an overarching participation on issues. They conclude with a warning:

> The future will be won by those who can spread their ideas better, faster, and more durably.... Those on the side of the angels, who want to spread compassion, promote pluralism, or defend science, must first grapple with a painful reality: that new power can supercharge hate and misinformation. In fact, those darker forces often start with an advantage because their provocations compel our attention and our clicks. It isn't enough to simply have the facts on your side.[30]

Companies need to adapt to the New Power phenomenon. The best defence against these threats is the embedded good habits of people who have learnt over the years to behave in a way that is consistent with the positive values of the company. No company can be protected from fraud, erosion of reputation and other risks unless it is consistent in its culture, in the sum total of all its behaviour and the messages which it communicates in all its relationships. This has become increasingly obvious as communication is now more instantaneous and international than ever. Since relationships overlap, and one can never know whether a particular audience comprises shareholders, taxpayers, regulators, suppliers as well as customers and employees, it is unwise to develop different messages, thinking that it is possible to compartmentalise them. A familiar example is how a company's chief executive would tell investors about the labour costs the firm would cut, while continuing to tell employees that they are the company's greatest assets. Such double talk is largely responsible for the cynicism that so many employees feel about the companies they work for.

One of the key features of companies that have survived over a long period of time is their ability to learn and adapt. Steward leaders know how to listen and so do their organisations. This equips them to anticipate risk, to sense changing attitudes and to be among the first to adapt.

Until a few years ago, no one would have imagined that companies might be criticised for trying to minimise their tax liabilities. But public attitudes change. As companies have become more open in claiming what good citizens they are, members of the public, including consumers, have started to ask how they reconcile that good citizenship with the measures they take to avoid paying tax in the countries where they sell their goods. One example is the pressure that was applied on Starbucks in the UK. In 2012, protesters occupied several Starbucks outlets and forced them to shut down temporarily, following the disclosure that Starbucks had paid only US$113 million in corporation tax in its fourteen years of trading in the UK and nothing in the last three years before the protest, citing no profit as a reason. The company had UK sales of nearly US$527 million in 2011 but had reported a taxable profit only once in its years of operating in the UK. In response to the ill-feeling, Starbucks even offered to pay a voluntary additional sum of over US$26 million a year over the next two years.[31]

Google's Eric Schmidt took a more defiant line, saying that he was proud of the company's tax-minimising arrangement, concluding with "that's capitalism".[32] It would have been more accurate to say "that's regulation". Capitalism is a much more flexible phenomenon, changing over time in response to the expectations of people in all their relationships. Attitudes change over time and successful companies anticipate and even lead the change. In this instance, Schmidt was not considering the (informal) "licence to operate" that accompanies the more formal tax rules.

The history of broken reputations is often a list of companies which have failed to understand that their (informal) "licence to operate" is shaped not just by government rules but also by public expectations. Companies will have to adapt, or at least be aware of how these are changing. The most successful will be those who can anticipate how their "licence to operate" is going to change with time. Gradually, yesterday's societal issue becomes today's customer concern.

All this has important implications for the approach companies take with regard to their communication strategies. The machine-age, top-down approach needs to be replaced with something more trusting and agile.

A Win-Win Approach

In Chapter 1, we discussed three views of the company. The shareholder primacy view leads people to ask why companies spend more than the absolute minimum of shareholders' money on looking after their employees or investing in their communities or the environment. This is a zero-sum way of thinking. Steward leaders reverse the question. If relationships are indeed the source of a company's success, then how can any company justify neglecting the health of its relationships with customers, employees, suppliers and society? How can shareholders justify ignoring the health of these relationships when they are the early warning system for future risks and opportunities? Why are organisations spending so little time on developing staff talent, monitoring opportunities and risks in their communities and their supply chains? The solution is in a win-win approach: the future success of business will be intertwined with the future success of society and that of the environment. Wealth is created in companies, and anyone involved in the ownership or leadership of companies needs to be focused on purpose, values and relationships as the true foundations for future growth. In the next three chapters, we will look more closely at the joint responsibility of the owners and the board in ensuring that this is indeed the focus for the company's leaders.

Chapter 4

From Investment Chain to Stewardship Value Chain

T he chairman of a listed company was reflecting on the boom years leading to the 2008 financial crisis. He regretted that he had failed to resist the pressure from institutional shareholders to increase the company's debt and pay out more to those shareholders. This decision left the company dangerously exposed when the cost of credit increased. He did not think it was the right thing to do at the time. He just did not know how to resist. He felt he had failed in his stewardship.

Such short-term thinking is costly to companies, investors and economies. As Dominic Barton and Mark Wiseman pointed out in a 2015 article for the *Financial Times*, the pressure to meet quarterly earnings targets has been estimated to have reduced research and development (R&D) spending and cut US growth by 0.1 percentage point a year.[1]

In contrast, stewardship is about having a long-term perspective. It is about building enduring companies which are the cornerstone of any economy. These will be companies that build a sustainable human existence by ensuring needs are met, creating workplace communities in which people can find challenge and fulfilment, paying salaries, dividends and taxes, and building infrastructure that contributes to the environment.

If companies are to live up to this potential, there needs to be joint effort between the management, board and owners. Together, these decision makers need to act as stewards, and have the joint responsibility of keeping the company on course. It falls especially on the asset owners, pension funds and other institutions, from whom savings flow into investments, to ensure that value is properly and fully defined and pursued so that companies can continue to grow. All of these market participants form part of a value chain. The wealth created through the system will be the result of the sum total of their efforts and behaviour.

Markets and the structure of law are like the hardware of our wealth creation. In many countries, attempts have been made to change the hardware without producing a different result. They are producing an increasingly unacceptable result.

The hardware can always be improved. But it is not so much the hardware that is the problem but the software, that is a combination of attitudes and behaviours that needs to change. Government interventions, investor incentives, boardroom behaviours, leadership choices and stakeholder pressure are all part of the answer but none will work in isolation. In their combined effect, they are the software. We need a different software, a different spirit. In effect, a coherent set of practices that are faithful to and aligned with the principles of stewardship is needed.

This chapter describes and discusses the investment chain that links the key actors. It asks, in particular, whether the current system is intelligent enough in interpreting the wishes of the clients and beneficiaries of the investment system. It considers how that chain might operate better for the benefit of companies, investors and citizens by encouraging the growth and continued success of dynamic and sustainable companies. Building on this, Chapters 5 and 6 then describe the stewardship actions that company boards and investment institutions might need to take in order to contribute to that success.

The first step towards progress is to recognise the core message of stewardship which is that those who are entrusted with assets or wealth of any kind have an obligation to hand those assets over in a better shape than when they received them. This obligation to be a good steward applies to everyone in the entire investment and wealth-creation chain — investors, entrepreneurs, shareholders, asset managers, as well as directors, managers, employees, analysts and advisors.

On the upstream end of the value chain, individual savers put money into savings or investment accounts. They contribute to pension schemes. They take out life insurance policies. They invest directly in mutual funds and other retail investment offerings. Their money could then take one of two routes. The first route is via a consolidated asset owner like a pension fund or a life fund. The people whose savings are being invested via this route are treated as beneficiaries. Someone else (say, a body of trustees) takes decisions in the saver's best interests. Advised by investment consultants and often by actuaries, that asset owner then develops an investment policy. To implement the policy, it contracts to asset managers whose specialisation is to decide where and how to invest the money to deliver the agreed returns.

The second route is more direct, and the individual whose savings are being invested is best described as a client or customer. The mutual funds collect the money from the clients, and make their own direct investment through asset managers who may be in-house or a third party. For the clients of life insurance policies, the chain is less clearly visible, but somewhere in the insurance company is a committee or body with responsibility for deciding how clients'

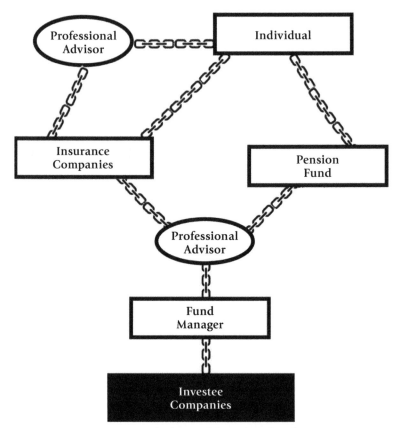

Figure 2: The "Stewardship Value Chain"

assets should be invested, as well as what degree of stewardship should be exercised.

Thus, smaller savings pots are combined into larger funds. These larger funds can be broken down into two types — the active funds and indexed funds. Active fund managers purchase particular company shares and exercise judgement in selecting firms whose growth prospects impress them or whose current share price seems to be at a good value. Indexed fund managers invest in all the shares in a defined index of companies, such as the FTSE 100 and hold on to those shares during the entire duration of time that the company remains in the index. Because the selection process is automatic, indexed funds have lower fees.

Savers' money does not always follow this route to investment in a range of stocks on the stock market. Part of it may go to property or real estate and be invested in shopping centres, big housing schemes, gold, silver or other commodities. Alternatively, part of it may go to private equity, a form of investment where a company that is not listed on a stock exchange accepts investments from specialist investors to help it grow, very often with the intention of it being sold later on.

A large proportion of the funds will end up in listed companies which are companies publicly quoted on stock exchanges where shares are traded every day. A huge investment research industry exists to support those asset managers in their work, analysing the company's accounts and comparing its current share price with what the analyst believes to be its underlying value or growth potential.

The asset manager, also known as the fund manager, is therefore the key link in the chain between the company and the ultimate investor. This is where the length and complexity of the investment chain begin to cause problems. The signals become too weak. If one talks to finance directors or chairmen or CEOs of investee companies, they will refer to the fund manager as their "investor". They do not have a line of sight to the ultimate investor, the original saver. In the eyes of the company, the asset manager *is* the investor. Strictly speaking, this asset manager is but an intermediary, whose stewardship responsibility is to represent the interests and wishes of the ultimate client or beneficiaries. Too often, in the pursuit of short-term investment performance, asset managers forget that they exist to serve clients who may have little interest in the quarterly ups and downs but are, in many cases, investing to achieve a return for their retirement decades later.

Whether a company is publicly listed or privately owned, shareholders elect the board of directors. The directors, under the leadership of the board chairman, appoint the CEO and stand at the apex of the company's leadership.

Looking through the lens of responsible wealth creation, a person or entity entrusted with funds throughout this system is a steward. Each of them has been put in place by someone before them in the investment chain with the responsibility to protect and enhance the assets. Each participant in the value chain entrusts that responsibility to the next — saver to asset owner, asset owner to asset manager, asset manager to company board. The company in turn makes investment decisions, entrusting funds to subsidiaries and divisions whose managers are then stewards of the funds under management. If the wealth-creation system as a whole is to function effectively and responsibly, it needs this investment chain to operate as a stewardship value chain.

Additionally, there are also, of course, wealthy individuals, family offices and foundations which are investing in the legacies of the past. For them, the stewardship obligation is more tangible. Wealth managers will always ask high-net worth clients what they want out of their investment. The same principle should apply to savers of modest means, and this is one of the key changes that will occur only when the savings and investment chain truly reflects stewardship principles. Then there are the enterprises owned by the state, and there are the sovereign wealth funds, that is, investments made by governments on behalf of their citizens and their future social security.

In crude terms, the investment community needs to recognise that the ultimate shareholders are all of us who save beyond the confines of our own community or family. Citizens are therefore also shareholders, except maybe the very poorest who do not have the resources to make the initial investment. Beyond their financial stake, the well-being of citizens is associated with the success or failure of the wealth creation system. Therefore, it can be said that the savings and investment system is there to serve citizens. It is directly accountable to those who have a financial stake, and is morally accountable to every citizen. This also means that throughout this process, the investment priorities of the individual or the group of individuals cannot be taken for granted. It is too superficial to say, as many people assume, that the client is only interested in making as much money as possible in the short term. Everyone wants a return. But at what cost, in terms of risk and impact? In an effective stewardship value chain, every investment fund in question will make clear its investment objectives, its time horizon and its approach to assessing whether the company is capable of making lasting returns. Investors who try to present investment priorities as a choice between ethics and superior financial returns are deceiving themselves and misleading their clients. Stewardship involves a search for approaches that will equip a company to make long-term returns while meeting the wider expectations of savers and investors.

Fund managers and other intermediaries need to take the trouble to find out and understand what the investors at each link of the chain want from all dimensions of their investment. This is the key change needed if the savings and investment system is indeed to be turned into a stewardship system. It boils down to two concepts which need to be defined at each link in the chain, and which need to reverberate throughout all discussions of stewardship — mandate and value.

A Joint Responsibility of Investors and Boards

The imagery of the investment chain is helpful in reminding us how the money flows from individual savers to companies but it would be misleading to imply that the chain only works in a single direction. It is equally important to look at the chain through the eyes of a company seeking finance. An entrepreneur starts a business and may borrow money from family, friends or the bank. The business grows and the entrepreneur, now a CEO, has a board of directors who have been elected by shareholders. The initiative for growth and the impetus of decision-making come from the executive, and the providers of capital hold the executive to account. Shrewd

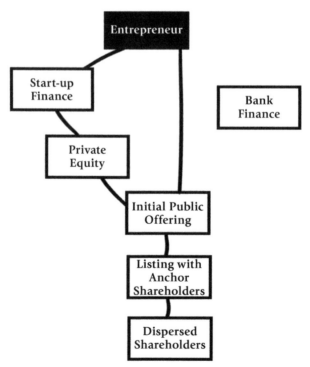

Figure 3: The Entrepreneur's Ownership Journey

entrepreneurs who have taken their company public do not sit back and wait to see which investors turn up. They set out their approach and seek out the types of backers who understand and believe in what they are trying to achieve. Imagine a successful entrepreneur who has taken the company public and has reduced his or her own shareholding to under 5 per cent. He needs to show respect and accountability to the shareholders who elect the board. That does not mean that the company is better served if that CEO becomes more passive and is cowed by the shareholders who dominate the share register. On the contrary, it is in everyone's interest that the entrepreneurial drive which saw the company grow in the first place is maintained.

The proper exercise of stewardship is thus a joint effort between companies and their owners, and the connecting mechanism between them is the board and the governance arrangements around the board. There is only so much the management of any business can achieve, unless the business owners and managers are fully aligned in their intent and appreciation of value.

Fiduciary Duty

So much for the value-chain map — as seen by the individual saver at one end, and the entrepreneur and business initiator at the other. But what about the obligations of the participants in between? The term "fiduciary duty" is central to an understanding of the stewardship of companies by boards and investors. However, it is often misunderstood and even misused, sometimes for reasons of self-interest.

The word *fiduciary* has the same Latin origins as the word *confidence*. It applies to someone who has been trusted or entrusted with a particular role to take care of particular assets. Thus, the Oxford English Dictionary defines it as "one who holds anything in trust". From its origins in a word that has everything to do with trustworthy behaviour, it has at times been twisted into an excuse for any behaviour that enhances opportunistic profit-making and self-enrichment within the technical boundaries of the law. For instance, in 2018, Nostrum Laboratories, a privately-owned pharmaceutical company, more than quadrupled the price of a bottle of antibiotics and defended the price hike, arguing there was a "moral requirement to sell the product at the highest price…. This is a capitalist economy and if you can't make money, you can't stay in business".[2]

Fiduciary duty is, in simple terms, the duty of being a steward or a trustee. Anyone who has a fiduciary duty must think and use his or her judgement to decide how to fulfil that duty. That involves balancing many considerations and often striking the right course between conflicting claims. It does not mean shutting down your conscience in the belief that you have a duty to maximise profits in any way that is legal. Fiduciary duty extends all the way along the value chain that connects savers and investors with companies. Let us consider here the fiduciary duty of the investor, and then that of the board.

Fiduciary duty of the investor

At the start of the stewardship value chain, there is usually, but not always, an individual who seeks to benefit from an investment. That person may be an individual shareholder directly investing in his or her own portfolio of shares, a beneficiary of one of several different types of pension funds, or a client of a mutual fund.

Sometimes, the investment is being made on behalf of a large body of individuals. For example, the original (ultimate) beneficiary might be the citizen of a country which has a state investment fund. Sometimes, the investment is being made on behalf of a wealthy family, where the client is a family office; sometimes, it is being made for the benefit of a charity or foundation. At other times, it is a commercial investment by a company whose business requires investment — for example, a life insurance company or a property firm.

The issue becomes complicated when there are more links in the chain, but the logic is the same. The ultimate beneficiaries or clients have the opportunity (which they often fail to take) to issue instructions to their fiduciaries about the returns they want from their investment, and the impact, behaviours and risks they would prefer to see associated with that investment. In other words, there needs to be a discussion about how the client defines value.

That then leads to the generation of a mandate. The pension fund or another collective fund then delegates the task of investing its assets to an asset manager (sometimes described as a fund manager). At this point, in the investment chain, there is the opportunity to specify the nature of the investment, and in turn, set the boundaries within which asset managers hold accountable the directors whom they, as shareholders, are responsible for electing or nominating. Corporate governance codes do not stop people from using this opportunity. Failure to do so is a failure of will (or ignorance).

Throughout this process, the investment priorities of the individual or the group of individuals cannot be taken for granted in their definition of what represents value. It is too superficial to say that the client is only interested in making as much money as possible, quarter by quarter. It is of course possible to generalise about earning them a return, and the fund in question will make it clear whether its focus is on growth or income. Equally, as the funds become consolidated, it is obviously impossible to satisfy every whim within a large and diverse group of individual beneficiaries. Generalisations have to be made about the kind of investment performance that is to be expected from an asset management fund. These generalisations will extend to what has become popularly known as ESG (Environmental, Social and Governance) considerations. Investors increasingly expect companies to be well-governed, mindful of health, safety and human rights, and, at the very least, aware of the risks associated with the environment. As the International Corporate Governance Network (ICGN) Model Mandate demonstrates, one thing above all needs to figure in the discussion about priorities, and that is time horizon. Good steward investors start by defining over what time horizon the client needs a return, and this gives them a much clearer sense of the kind of investments likely to achieve this.[3]

Then, there is the role of indexed funds. Indexed funds are cheaper but once one has chosen to invest in such a fund, one is accepting a package of all the companies which form that index. However, since the asset manager is committed to the company the whole time it stays in the index, there is all the more reason to try and influence the behaviour of some or all the companies in the index, especially those which may be departing most strongly from the ultimate investors' priorities. (For this reason, it is a mistake to confuse indexation with passive investing. The best index investors are highly active).

So, overall, in order to do justice to their fiduciary duty, steward investors must undertake two tasks. The first is to find out as far as is practical what the individual or individuals see as desirable investment performance. In other words, how do they as shareholders interpret value? The other is to factor into the investment criteria the issues which will have an impact not only on the value of the investment but also on the ability of beneficiaries to enjoy its fruits. Both tasks can be performed by a single asset manager, but the second will be performed more effectively by a number of investment institutions working together and exercising a more powerful stewardship influence.

There are always boundaries and qualifications. Here we are talking only about investments that are legal — money laundering and drug cartels are out. Next, there is the question of time horizon. Over what time period does the individual need the money earned or returned? Three months? A year? A decade?

Next, there is the question of ethics, behaviours and impact. What impact do individuals want to make, or avoid, as a result of this investment? None? Or are they happy to leave it to the investment professionals to tell them what is best? Or to screen out certain products like tobacco or guns? Or does the individual want to prioritise funds which have a positive impact on the environment?

Next, there is the question of the kind of companies the money is invested in. Does the individual want to give priority or perhaps the entire investment to companies that have a track record of treating their people well, training them, offering opportunities to others from minority or disadvantaged backgrounds?

The crude view of fiduciary duty, implying that every beneficiary of investment wants the same thing, and that short-term financial measurement adequately describes what they want, is very convenient for asset managers and other intermediaries. It allows them to simplify their business model and marketing and focus purely on short-term financial returns. They can concentrate on the claim that their fund has been in the top ten for the last two years without mentioning the collateral damage they have caused from constant pressure on companies to drive shareholder value over the short term even if that is at the expense of future performance.

It is hard for anyone to ignore the effects of volatile stock prices and the running commentary of sell-side analysts whose job is to find or create stories around the over- or under-valuation of a company's shares. Rightly or wrongly, the idea that companies listed on public markets are earnings machines has taken root in the public psyche. The market expects profits, and wants to see evidence of progress towards these profits every quarter. Yet, in this context, *the market* is a fiction. Clients and beneficiaries are real people. They have their own priorities and expectations and it is the job of investment professionals, like any other professional, to find out what they are, not speculate about what they might be.

Most asset managers are not that simplistic or short-term. Yet, overall, CEOs of listed companies will privately admit that they face relentless pressure to grow earnings and feed the hungry beast of the capital markets. And so, beneath the surface of easy statements in the name of fiduciary duty, lies a dangerous contradiction. In their apparent pursuit of shareholder value, institutional investors are often contributing to a system that is knowingly or unknowingly undermining the stewardship of the companies that generate long-term shareholder value. They can only be good stewards if they pay attention to their impact. If, by their actions, they create a climate of short-termism, they are unwittingly limiting the ability of their companies to create value for their clients.

Even taking the most exclusive and narrow approach to the problem, if the owners and providers of financial capital are to protect the financial value of their investments into the future, they have to safeguard the natural, human and financial capital with which nature and previous generations have endowed them. The financial success of the businesses in which they invest depends on the continuing availability of this capital. Businesses need the stability that comes from the legal system, from traditions of decent behaviour, from the everyday effectiveness of the banking system and other utilities in oiling the wheels of the economy. It is impossible for shareholders to separate the value of their investment from an assessment of the condition of these related capitals.

This argument was reinforced recently in a *Harvard Business Review* essay by Oliver Hart and Luigi Zingales:

> We offer a different perspective, one that we believe is perfectly consistent with the fiduciary duties of corporate directors: Companies should maximise shareholder *welfare*, not value. Our starting point is that shareholders care about more than just money. Many shareholders pay more for fair-trade coffee, or buy electric cars rather than cheaper gas guzzlers, because, using the current economic lingo, they are *prosocial*. They care, at least to some degree, about the health of society at large. Why would they not want the companies they invest in to behave similarly?[4]

Enlightened investors recognise all of this. Yet, it is very difficult to influence any one company to change its behaviour accordingly when, as is usually the case with listed companies, the largest investor owns but a small percentage of the shares. It requires collaboration with others, and to achieve improvement, it may well require applying that collective influence to a whole industry, and not just one company in isolation. This leads to a third aspect of fiduciary duty — the obligation of investment institutions, where practical, to work in concert with one another in the best interest of their clients and beneficiaries. Such coordination will be welcomed by the leaders and boards of those listed companies which complain about the difficulty they have in getting the attention of their shareholders. This leads naturally to fiduciary duty as it is seen by the company.

Fiduciary duty of the board

For stewardship to be effective, it needs another key perspective of fiduciary duty — that of the company. How should businesses and their boards respond to the differing motivations of different groups of shareholders? How can the board achieve greater cohesion among shareholders and thus enhance the chances of effective joint stewardship by these shareholders and boards?

The principle is the same. Under most forms of company law around the world, directors owe their duty to the company, not to shareholders. The board is, in most systems, elected by shareholders. But that does not mean that directors are there to follow every whim of every shareholder. Nor does it mean that the board is there only to maximise shareholder value. Once again, the two key concepts are value and mandate. As good stewards and fiduciaries, directors have a duty to promote the success of the company. By doing that, they will create value for shareholders. They have to find the right balance between results today and results in the future. In the previous chapter, we explained that one of the principal tasks of steward leaders is to define what success means for the company, in light of its unique purpose and values. In a mature company, this will be set and reviewed in dialogue between executive and non-executives on the board. The board, in other words, needs to work out what its mandate is. This task will be described in detail in Chapter 5. The board may, and should, listen to the shareholders by whom it was elected, and the creation of a board mandate will give clarity to those conversations. The board is not there to take instructions from any one group of shareholders, large or small. Instead, it has been put in place to exercise its judgement in the best interest of the company.[5]

As mentioned before, fiduciary duty is used as an argument to defend short-termism and the "plundering" of a company for the benefit of immediate shareholders. Yet, this has no basis in law. As the late Professor Lynn Stout, a professor of corporate and business law at Cornell Law School, puts it:

> There is a common belief that corporate directors have a legal duty to maximise corporate profits and 'shareholder value' — even if this means skirting ethical rules, damaging the environment or harming employees. But this belief is utterly false.

Professor Stout says that corporate case law "describes directors as fiduciaries who owe duties not only to shareholders but also to the corporate entity itself, and instructs directors to use their powers in 'the best interests of the company'".

She reminds us that serving shareholders' "best interests" is not the same thing as maximising profits or maximising shareholder value. "Shareholder value", for one thing, is a vague objective. No single "shareholder value" can exist, because different shareholders have different values. Some are long-term investors planning to hold stock for years or decades, while others are short-term speculators.[6]

In a recent commentary, governance and UK law expert Paul Lee reinforces Stout's argument by examining the two cases which have been quoted in support of a narrower interpretation of the board's fiduciary duty — Dodge versus Ford Motor Company[7] and eBay versus Newmark.[8] Neither ruling says that the law stops directors from taking the broadest view of their duties. It is the directors' own choice.[9] [10] Lee states that in both cases, the issue was that it was the interests of minority shareholders that had been side-lined. For both the US and the UK, the law "commends attention being paid to stakeholder interests beyond a narrow understanding of shareholder value maximisation".[11] However, regrettably, the board tends to focus just on the "narrowest possible understanding of their role".[12]

Thus, the very same stewardship priorities which are needed for institutional investors apply equally to company boards. Be clear about your mandate — your formal mandate from the shareholders who elected you, and your informal "licence to operate" from society. In short, define your purpose. Clarify what you mean by value and success, and then measure and report accordingly. There may have to be a parting of ways in situations where shareholders and the company's purpose and long-term plans are not aligned.

Fiduciary duty is not an alibi for corporate or investor ruthlessness. It is an obligation that can only be fulfilled by good stewardship. The stewardship value chain is only as strong as its weakest link. The stewardship of a company is therefore, the joint responsibility of all actors along the chain. In that regard, stewardship is like a thread which needs to be woven, through the behaviours and responsibilities of all involved. In Chapters 5 and 6, we will delve deeper into the stewardship role of boards and investors respectively.

Chapter 5

The Board as Steward

The company is a living system. Employees are its life-blood. Management is the heart which keeps the blood pumping. Strategy is the brain. Measurement and communication are the central nervous system. Culture is the DNA. Leadership and continued entrepreneurial energy are its soul and spirit. Governance and accountability are its rhythms and disciplines. Like exercise, they are a means of keeping this living organism fit and lean. Unless we understand governance in this wide context, we will continually fail to manage risk, sustain performance and earn trust.[1]

Corporate governance is greatly misunderstood, and at times, more harm than good has been done in its name. Governance has its place, but it should not be allowed to stand in the way of innovation and entrepreneurial flair. It has become over-complicated and over-prescriptive. Yet, in essence, it is very simple. It is a set of arrangements for keeping companies honest and accountable. Corporate governance codes are usually intended to be voluntary. They have been designed that way to save businesses from prescriptive and intrusive legislation. They are there to ensure companies chart their own course within clear limits.

The problem is that often people forget about the spirit of the codes and concentrate on what they think is their obligation to follow every letter. The problem is compounded, in many regulatory regimes, by an artificial separation between the expectations placed upon directors and those placed upon investors, treating the two as if they exist in separate universes, when both are actually involved in joint stewardship of companies. Corporate governance is only as good as the stewardship context in which it operates.

Corporate governance exists to keep companies honest, focused, safe, healthy and accountable. Directors are the stewards in charge, entrusted by owners, shareholders and investors to take care of the assets and hand them on to their successors in a better condition. In fulfilling their responsibilities, they need to see the company as a living system. In order to fulfil their stewardship responsibilities, directors need to behave like owners. As owners, shareholders also need to behave like stewards. While this chapter focuses on the role of boards, Chapter 6 focuses on the role of asset owners and asset managers. Stewardship is a joint responsibility of all.

The stewardship view of governance incorporates the three key stewardship elements that were described in Chapter 2. Firstly, stewardship intent (will), that is, being proactive and focusing on the spirit rather than the letter of governance codes. Secondly, integrating present and future, managing the short-term and meeting the expectations of today's shareholders and stakeholders, but also making the right decisions today for the long term so that in time, the business is handed over in a better condition for the benefit of tomorrow's shareholders and stakeholders. And thirdly, understanding interdependence. Directors need to understand their place in the stewardship value chain — elected by and formally accountable to owners and shareholders, but owing their duty to the company and the health of all its relationships.

Priorities of Owners, Boards in Exercising Joint Stewardship

Because stewardship is a joint activity between the owners and the managers of the business, effective stewardship can be achieved only when there is a cohesive link between owners and managers. The practice of this joint stewardship involves four key areas of action by the board in partnership with the owners and shareholders. The initiative usually lies with the board because it is more hands-on than the shareholders. In a tightly controlled family business, the initiative may sometimes come from the family owners, but where there is a more dispersed ownership of shares, it is hard to coordinate with the shareholders. So, usually the board proposes and the shareholders dispose. The four areas of action are summarised below and accompanied by a series of questions that the board needs to ask itself.

Priority 1: Setting the course — clarity of purpose, roles and relationships

The first area of action is *clarity* of purpose, values, behaviours, relationships, the definition of value and success, roles and a good company mandate. Shareholders, directors and managers ought to have the same agenda for action, be clear about what is to be achieved, and by whom and who is accountable to whom.

In setting the course, the board can start by creating a board mandate. This sets out the expectations that the board has of itself, and the board's understanding of the expectations that shareholders and other key stakeholders have for the board and the company. The process of creating a board mandate forces directors to confront important questions:

- What is our authority? Who has put us here? What are we to achieve, and over what timeframe? What are the limits of our scope?

- What is our role? How does it relate to the role of our owners/shareholders, executive management, other panels or governance mechanisms, joint-venture partners, trade unions or societal partners?

- What is the organisation's purpose, values and behaviour? What do we stand for? Do we practise what we preach? How do we check? How do we define success and how do we reward performance?

- What is its strategy and business model? How far are we empowered to change this? Where are the potential conflicts of interest? What is our risk appetite?

The process of creating a mandate involves deep discussion by the board. It provides a basis for shared understanding of the fundamentals of the business. It is a common core which can act as a basis for engagement with shareholders, regulators, business partners, employees and NGOs. It enables the board to achieve integration. *(See Mandate toolkit at end of chapter)*. The experience of Barclays, the global banking group, shows what happens if the board has not clarified the mandate in this way.

> Everything we do starts with our customers. That may sound like a truism but we are in business to help them... There are certain basic principles that underpin

everything we do in relation to our customers. We should be open and transparent, we should ensure that our products always meet genuine needs.[2]

So reads the 2006 Corporate Responsibility report of Barclays. Around this time, Barclays Group was competing for awards in recognition of its corporate citizenship work in support of education and the community. When a senior executive in charge of corporate responsibility was making a presentation to the judges, he was asked one question that he could not answer. Do the same values that lie behind the good citizenship of the retail bank also apply to the way people behave in Barclays investment bank?

It later emerged that between 2005 and 2009, staff in the investment bank had colluded with other banks to manipulate the London Inter-Bank Offer Rate (LIBOR) to benefit its trading position. At least US$350 trillion in derivatives and other financial products were tied to LIBOR. In addition, between 2007 and 2009, the firm had made dishonestly low LIBOR submission rates to dampen market speculation and negative media comments about its viability during the financial crisis. In settling with UK and US regulators, the firm agreed to pay US$450 million in fines. Within a few days of the settlement, Barclays' CEO Robert Diamond resigned under pressure from British regulators.

This is how the 2013 Review into Barclays by leading lawyer Anthony Salz described what he found there:

> But the overriding purpose at Barclays in the lead-up to the crisis and beyond was expressed in terms of increases in revenues and profits, return on equity and competitive position. The drift in standards was manifest in the events that set the context for this Review. There was no

sense of common purpose in a group that had grown and diversified significantly in less than two decades. And across the whole bank, there were no clearly articulated and understood shared values, so there could hardly be much consensus among employees as to what the values were and what should guide everyday behaviour. And as a result, there was no consistency to the development of a desired culture…. there was an over-emphasis on short-term financial performance, reinforced by remuneration systems that tended to reward revenue generation rather than serving the interests of customers and clients.[3]

If only the board of Barclays had been through a thorough discussion of its mandate from investors, and the mandate that they, in turn, set for senior executives. What if the non-executive directors on the board of Barclays had asked that same awkward question, that is: "These values about customer focus and transparency sound good, but do we apply them everywhere, and how do we check?"

Priority 2: Driving performance — attention to continual improvement

It is pointless if a company wins good governance awards in one year, only to go out of business the next. This joint action concerns the discipline of operations, but it is more than that. It means maintaining the energy and drive for improvements that are to be found in all enduring and successful companies, an effort that involves all stakeholders. Leaders and managers must routinely review performance, always with the proviso that the pursuit of results should never override the correct behaviours that must accompany the firm's values. They need to stimulate all kinds of innovation and institute performance-improvement programmes. The board has the advantage of standing back, and its non-executive members have wide experience which they can use to stimulate more lateral thinking about the way things are done, the market opportunities, and the potential for new partnerships and initiatives.

Two examples illustrate this — one from a small-time business, and the other from a large one. In *Timeless Ventures*, a study of long-lived companies in Japan (cited in Chapter 2), Haruo Funabashi writes about a small family blacksmith business that has survived for over 750 years. It has survived through constant adaptation and improvement. The family business started by making armour for feudal lords. As the weapons used in battle changed from swords and spears to firearms, the family had to adapt their armour accordingly. Then came a period of peace where protective armour was largely used during ceremonial occasions, and suddenly, the product had to be lighter. Then, at the end of the feudal era, armour was no longer needed. The business had to further adapt their technology to making tongs and farm implements. The Second World War forced the family temporarily out of business, but after the war, they hit on the idea of making wind chimes. As Funabashi puts it:

> Under the most trying conditions, these small sets of blacksmiths had to turn over their expertise, change skills and adapt to new products because they were demanded by people... What makes this company long-lived ...is their spirit of togetherness and values that helped them change.[4]

The Toyota Way, a set of principles and behaviours, and indeed, the Toyota production system is the embodiment of this stewardship priority. Fujio Cho, Toyota's president, said in 2002:

We place the highest value on implementation and taking action. There are many things one doesn't understand and therefore, we ask them why don't you just go ahead and take action; try to do something? You realise how little you know and you face your own failures and you simply can correct those failures and redo it again and at the second trial you realise another mistake and another thing you didn't like so you can redo it once again. So, by constant improvement, or should I say, the improvement based upon action, one can rise to the higher level of practice and knowledge.[5]

Matching deeds with words is a crucial task of leadership. Nowhere is this more true than in matters of remuneration and its relationship with performance. The board and its leaders often show their true colours in the way they define and reward the performance of others, and how they themselves are paid. Since leaders should not determine their own pay, this becomes a vital part of the board's role. In this regard, many of the most advanced economies have created an enormous mess with regard to pay. Research by Andrew Smithers charted the consequences in terms of higher profitability and lower investment:

The change in remuneration, which dates in the US from around 1992, coincided with the change in corporate behaviour. The correlation between corporate returns on equity and tangible investment as a percentage of output … has since been statistically insignificant. Incentives are designed to change behaviour and we should not therefore be surprised at the marked change in corporate behaviour that has followed the dramatic change in incentives. Quoted companies have recently been investing around half as much as unquoted companies though the two groups appear of equal importance to the economy. As today's perverse incentives apply most strongly to quoted companies, this provides additional evidence for attributing low investment to the malign impact of the bonus culture. Increasing investment and growth thus requires that we reform management remuneration.[6]

From this analysis, board decision-makers have neglected the stewardship priorities when deciding on the remuneration of senior executives. First, there has been a failure of clarity about what motivates people to achieve. The flawed underlying premise, spoken or unspoken, is that financial success is the only sort of success, and that financial rewards are the only kind of rewards that will motivate people, especially when time horizons are too short. As a result, the true focus on progressive performance improvement is replaced by an obsession with sacrificing the future health of the business for visible short-term gains. Such arrangements may unwittingly incentivise people to *game* the system and not focus their efforts on the long-term best interests of the company. In listed companies, they have made the problem worse by trying to "align the interests of managers with those of shareholders", when there is no common set of interests for shareholders except the creation of long-term value for the company. Rewards are usually linked to the company's share price or profitability. It may encourage the company to put the long-term health of the business at risk so as to pander to the interests of a small number of executives and a group of short-term shareholders. The sum total of all these misjudgements is a failure of companies to sense or shape the wider landscape. This has led employees in many companies to become cynical and mistrustful of the business and what their leaders have to say.

The usual approach to remuneration still tends to be based on the belief that enhancing financial incentives will lead to better performance. There is research which throws doubt on this belief. Daniel Pink's research, quoted in Chapter 3, concludes that bigger incentives have led to worse performances.[7] Professor Dan Ariely and his colleagues from MIT have raised the possibility that (beyond a certain point), increased incentives in a variety of tasks, especially cash, tend to have an adverse effect on employee performance.[8] Professor Ariely explains that financial incentives can produce a "long-term disassociation" where employees question whether money is the only reason why they work in lieu of a deeper purpose.[9] This seems especially true of activities involving cognitive skills as opposed to physical effort.

The areas of business where large rewards are offered and rapid decisions are made tend to be the trading floors or other dealmaking environments. Likewise, in the world of mergers and acquisitions, practitioners talk about the psychology of "deal fever" and the failure of companies to be critical about the fees they are paying. Decisions made under such pressure, where great riches beckon if a deal is made, are unlikely to appropriately balance the long-term consequences of the deal with the people involved in it, whether now or in the future. Meanwhile, it appears that the incentives for mergers and acquisitions are not linked to the long-term value that is created in the merged entity. The remuneration rationale is disconnected from the logic of creating long-term value.

It is hardly surprising that boards and executives who are accustomed to such a world bring some of the same practices to their decision-making regarding the remuneration of top executives.

And for the same top executives, the problem is compounded by ambitious CEOs who want to be recognised, and if they think money is the best means by which that recognition is conferred, then they will want to be the best paid. The great companies are those where their senior executives enjoy what they feel to be fair rewards, but that alone is not what makes them want to stay. They stay because they enjoy, believe in, and are stretched by what they do. Their rewards are fair and are linked to purpose, values and the success model of the business. That is stewardship at work. That would help to encourage a business future in which companies can be left free to generate wealth, while earning the trust of their investors, staff and other stakeholders.

Priority 3: Sensing and shaping the landscape

The third priority is about being outward- and forward-looking. A common feature of all the companies that have survived and prospered over centuries is how connected they have been with the outside world. This determines how good they are at sensing both opportunity and risk.

This is the proper context for discussions about sustainability and corporate social responsibility. Not as a separate compartment, but as part of an integrated understanding of the world around the company and the company's place in, and contribution to, that world.

Boards need to have a good radar. They need to understand how society is changing and how that affects the business opportunities and risks that they will face. In recent years, there has been much emphasis on corporate governance codes and risk management, and rightly so. However, the problem with risk management is that, too often, it operates only at the level of checklists. The opportunity for better risk management lies in the ability of a company to receive and listen to feedback and look at itself in a new light.

BP's Texas City disaster, which killed fifteen people, illustrates this. In her book, *Wilful Blindness*, Margaret Heffernan reports that two of the key people involved in the errors leading up to the explosion had been working non-stop for 33 and 37 days, one of them on twelve-hour shifts. The BP board had been relentlessly focused on achieving 25 per cent cost cuts following the company's acquisition of Amoco, which owned Texas City's refinery. There had been many figures presented to the BP board about its successful cost-reduction programme. In hindsight, it turns out that repeated monitoring of cost reductions would have saved a lot less lives and money than monitoring overtime patterns, or asking to know more about how employees felt about how the programme was going. In the same way, board members who ask probing questions about bullying or sexual harassment before these issues appear all over social media are making a valuable contribution.[10]

Reputation, brand and long-term success are all at risk when a company fails to live by its purpose and values. In turn, these values and principles need to be in tune with the expectations of people outside the business, whether they are customers, neighbourhoods or the wider public. Hence, there is increasing importance placed by regulators on the governance of culture and the risks associated with it.[11] The board needs to be sensitive to culture and behaviour.

Priority 4: Planting for the future — coherence over time

This fourth joint action is about integrating the short and the long term. It is often complicated as the owners and managers of a business may not share the same time horizon and perspectives, let alone try to gel long-term and short-term interests. Every business has to manage its cash flow, balance income and expenditure by the week and the month. Stewardship is about ensuring the short term does not triumph at the expense of the long term. But business owners and managers need to decide what constitutes the right balance.

Often, it is the stewardship commitment to developing people for the benefit of society and community that proves to be the most concrete embodiment of this principle of planting for the future.

There could be few better illustrations of the importance of planting for the future than the contrasting stories of Unilever and Kraft, the company that attempted and failed to take over Unilever in 2017.

Paul Polman became CEO of Unilever in 2009. With the support of his board, Polman set out clear medium-term goals, together with the ambitious Unilever Sustainable Living Plan. He dropped quarterly reporting and quarterly earnings guidance, and invited shareholders who wanted a short-term approach to place their investments elsewhere. He explained: "I don't have any space for many of these people that really, in the short term, try to basically speculate and make a lot of money."[12]

In 2017, Kraft Heinz made a bid to take over Unilever. It is not entirely clear why, contrary to the shareholders of other bid targets, the shareholders of Unilever did not press the company to engage in merger talks with Kraft Heinz. In other cases of offers being made public, shareholders have certainly pressed boards to explore a deal and in effect ensured such transactions happened. But this did not happen in any significant way for the Kraft Heinz-Unilever case. Perhaps they were open to broader ideas of stewardship. Perhaps Polman's abandonment of the quarterly numbers game as his first public act as CEO had helped him attract more long-term minded shareholders. Perhaps some had an inkling that the apparently successful Kraft Heinz model might be tarnished. Whatever the reason, Polman had succeeded in planting for the future.

The contrast with Kraft Heinz is striking. In February 2019, the company announced a US$15 billion write-down of the value of its two most famous brands. It cut its dividend by more than 30 per cent and announced that its procurement was being investigated by the US Securities and Exchange Commission. Kraft Heinz was the product of a merger in 2015 between the two giants, Kraft and Heinz. The merger was backed by 3G, an aggressive private equity firm whose style was described by *The Economist* as "buy a big business, cut costs, repeat".[13] Fund managers and analysts were initially enthusiastic about the aggressive cost-cutting while suppliers took the brunt of management aggression. The company tried to show it could boost sales but failed, not least because, in the words of *The Economist*:

> Brands [such as Kraft Heinz] may be familiar, but that does not make them popular. Small firms are offering healthier options, taking advantage of cheap digital marketing and nimble contract manufacturers.... The notion that big deals will save American food firms looks increasingly dubious.[14]

Shares are now down by more than half since the Kraft and Heinz merger in 2015. Kraft Heinz is learning about the importance of the longer term. It should have been spending on R&D and marketing to revive its offerings, but its owner, 3G Capital, was focused solely on aggressively cutting corporate fat. As Rana Foroohar wrote in *The Financial Times*:

The company demonstrates how a strategy focused on short-term results can backfire…. Kraft Heinz has lost more than half its equity value since its creation in a 2015 merger…. You could come up with dozens of other timely, high-profile examples of companies that have stumbled after making Faustian bargains to please Wall Street.[15]

Perhaps Kraft Heinz would not be in this position if it had followed the advice of Unilever CEO Paul Polman:

Investors with a responsibility to generate long-term returns to match their pension liabilities had the same responsibility to ensure that their members 'are retiring in a world they can live in'.[16]

THE CHAIR AS STEWARD

Governance is a system. It is a system that is only as good as those who occupy the leading roles. Hence, the chair needs to be the very embodiment of stewardship intent.

In 1990, former McKinsey head Hugh Parker wrote *Letters to a New Chairman*. Twenty-five years later, drawing on extensive interviews with company chairs and their many stakeholders, Tomorrow's Company published a new edition, which described the chairman's role in these terms:

Every chairmanship is unique in that the business, the competitive circumstances, the pace of opportunities and risks that can go wrong, the unexpected crises that threaten you, the people you work with, and the culture of the organisation, are all different. The only single constant is your own character imprinted on all these. You have to set your own style and exercise your power with humanity. You are very visible, and need to be decisive when it matters. There are some obvious commonalities: the role of the board is to define and establish the purpose and values of the enterprise, and to guard and foster its reputation...The chairman's role is to hold all this together and champion the role of the board. Think of the conductor of an orchestra, who has many players contributing skills that he does not personally have, each with specialised and focused perspectives, knowledge and concerns, each required to participate at times and at volumes that only he sees in the full score. The chairman commands the tempo, the mood, the excitement by balance and priority of the parts through his own personality and style. That's your key role.[17]

With every corporate disaster, questions are asked about the board. Did it miss the obvious warning signs? Was it too complacent? Was it not diverse enough? Was it too narrowly focused on short-term performance and the share price? An indispensable role of the chairman as steward is to anticipate these challenges. The chair ensures that the board reviews its own performance, individually and collectively. This involves the chair discussing with board members the following:

- Do we have a culture where challenge is encouraged? Do we regularly review the effectiveness of our board? Do we do this formally? How do we review our own effectiveness as directors, both individually and collectively? Do we obtain feedback from one another and our chair?

- Are we happy with the role of the chair and the way he or she performs this role? Do we have regular meetings between individual members and the chair to ensure that there is mutual feedback? Do we have a senior independent director? Would such an appointment be helpful in dealing with concerns about the chair? Do we have sufficient independent directors able to offer an external perspective? Are we happy with the process of nominating new directors? Have we got the right balance between knowledge and experience on the one hand, and freshness and independence on the other?

- How well do we feel we did when performing the function of monitoring and reviewing the management, results, employee relationships, supply-chain relationships, shareholder relationships, relationships with and contribution to the community and future generations?

Last but not least, the chair provides a vital link in the stewardship value chain. In theory, although often not in practice, the chair is chosen by the shareholders or owners. When things go wrong, it is the chair to whom the major shareholders will go. In the next chapter, we explore how investors, especially institutional investors, may best operate to make both the selection of, and the dialogue with, the chair as fruitful as possible in promoting the success of the company.

LISTED COMPANIES AND DISPERSED SHAREHOLDING: A STEWARDSHIP VACUUM

One of the first things that the chair of a listed company may do upon appointment is to write to the top twenty institutions which hold shares in the company and offer to meet them. A few meetings may follow. Typically, many institutions will reply, saying that they see no need to meet at the present time, but will be in touch if this changes.

Though everyone in the value chain is a steward, the onus for steward-oriented leadership falls as a joint responsibility between shareholders and directors. The board represents the owners and needs to behave like steward leaders. But what if the owners of the shares fail to behave like stewards? Cohesion and communication between directors and shareholders are vital to the stability and leadership of the company. For stewardship to work, a critical mass of owners needs to be engaged and responsible. If everyone owns but a minute percentage of a company, there is little capacity or incentive for anyone to be a responsible owner. An engaged institutional investor may well ask: "Why should I do the heavy lifting when the benefits of my efforts are spread across a large group of investors who haven't lifted a finger to get involved?"

In listed companies, the dispersal of shareholding and the passivity of most shareholders have in the past combined to make it much easier for irresponsible CEOs to take undue risks or to negotiate unjustified remuneration packages without being restrained by their investors. And, with honourable exceptions, those investors who sense that the company was on an unsustainable path are likely to sell their holdings rather than work with others to put things right.

The dispersal of shareholding can undermine stewardship. The more dispersed the shareholding, the harder it is for the shareholders to act as an effective body capable of holding executives and the board to account, and to exercise stewardship. In a recent post, Goethe University's Professor Katja Langenbucher summarised the difficulties:

> Shareholders' interests vary greatly. We find shareholders betting on a corporation's stock price going down. We find others prepared to support measures which will lead to stock prices going up for the short-term only. We find shareholders uninterested in the corporation, holding shares only due to an index tracker or investment advice. We find yet others heavily invested in keeping a low-risk investment over a very long time span. Out of the broad spectrum of possible management strategies which every corporation faces, each option will cater more to the taste of some than of others.[18]

THREE RESPONSES

First response — seek out steward shareholders

As stewards of the company, the best boards insist that the firm seek out investors who have stewardship intent. They are usually the long-term investors which may include state-owned entities, sovereign wealth funds, pension funds, insurance companies, wealthy family and private group investors like Berkshire Hathaway. The board will want to know whether the company has sought to attract more steward investors so as to create stability of ownership and make stewardship more effective. What is the optimal proportion of the total share register that should be made up of steward investors? How can the board engage the steward investors to help the company think about issues of future appointment of non-executive directors and CEO succession?

Second response — involve shareholders in the board nomination process

There has been one particularly effective innovation in Europe which has helped to achieve a more thorough involvement of institutional investors while still respecting the rights of smaller shareholders. This is the Swedish system of nomination committees.

The asset managers who hold shares in listed companies on our behalf are busy people. They may hold hundreds or thousands of shares around the world. When time is short, delegation is essential. The key to good delegation by big investors is to ensure that the right board is in place so as to be good stewards of the business. But in modern stock markets, one often finds that the largest shareholder holds only 1 or 2 per cent of the shares. In such a scenario, there is no natural sense of stewardship where one can actually gather a significant chunk of owners in the room. What good stewardship needs is disparate shareholders working together. This is difficult. It needs to be made easier, and the larger of those investors need to make it more of a priority, especially in the key issue of director nomination.

The chairs of some listed companies seem to have the power to nominate directors with all the imperiousness of a Maharajah. They are often heard saying that the decision to appoint new directors must be the chair's because the chair is responsible for the effective operation of the board. Such a statement flies in the face of the legal position. Under company law, the shareholders elect the directors.

In most companies, there is a board nomination committee whose task is to vet candidates and guide the process, but this remains strictly a board process. Too often, it is a formal endorsement of the wishes of the chair. Even when there is more independent thinking in the nomination committee, the process is in danger of creating a self-perpetuating oligarchy. Directors today seem to decide who their new colleagues should be, and then put their nomination through the formality of the shareholder vote. With shareholding so dispersed and passive, the directors are the ones who propose and the shareholders "rubber-stamp" the choice.

In Sweden, however, there is a different approach which encourages greater stewardship. The board nomination committee is formed by representatives of the largest investors in the company. The chairman of the company attends, but does not chair this nomination committee. The result is that major institutions can come together to work as stewards of a company in the most important task, that is, ensuring that it has the right board. The Swedes were inspired, ironically, by the report in the UK by Sir Adrian Cadbury in 1992 on the financial aspects of corporate governance.[19] On reviewing their system in light of this report, they moved away from the self-perpetuating oligarchy whereby an existing board of directors or a current chairman is responsible for choosing their successors. They decided that since the formal expectation under company law is that directors are chosen by investors, they should set up an investor-led nomination committee, on which all the major (steward) investors sit.[20]

Interestingly, the circumstances which prompted the Swedes to act in this way were not unlike those often found in Asia. Sweden had at the time a number of companies with a dominant shareholder, and there was a desire to ensure that minority shareholders were treated fairly and had a proper say in the selection of the board. For instance, India has several promoter-controlled companies, and again, there are legitimate concerns that the rights of minority shareholders may not be properly respected.

In principle, there is nothing to stop any listed company from implementing the arrangements which operate in Sweden. The rules could be framed to ensure that minority shareholders are fairly represented on the nomination committee. Where there are shareholder organisations set up to represent individual shareholders, they too could be granted a representative on the nomination committee. This could prove a valuable way of gathering shareholders who have a common concern and a stewardship orientation, getting them to come together to select the right board. In companies and countries where trade unions represent the legitimate voice of employees who have no formal right of representation, they too could be offered a place on the nomination committee. Where employees have shares in the company, they too could be offered a place on the nomination committee.

In practice, just as the Swedish system evolved in stages, it might therefore, make sense for listed companies to experiment first by inviting major (engaged and responsible) shareholders to nominate representatives to serve on their nomination committees. The most important learning point from the Swedish experience is that the nomination process is a good catalyst for bringing together the major investors to make a shared assessment of the company's situation, as well as for working together in a more proactive way than is experienced at present.

Third response — a planned, progressive shift towards more stable ownership

Many of the most enduring companies have designed their structure in ways which ensure stability of ownership. Tata and Sons is a good example. Over 150 years on from its formation, Tata has survived and thrived by combining stable ownership by family trusts at the group level, with individual companies below group level, each of which is a major firm in its own right with stock market listing, but with Tata and Sons holding a significant shareholding.

Tata and Sons may be a great example, but it is the product of a unique vision faithfully pursued over generations. Listed company boards battling conflicting demands of dispersed shareholding might ask themselves how they can solve the problem without Tata's unique history and constitution. It is important to challenge the assumption that a company's ownership and business form are unchangeable.[21]

Handelsbanken is an example of this dynamic approach to business form.[22] Handelsbanken is a prudent and successful bank which survived the global financial crisis without a bailout. Its belief in long-termism has helped bring about this result.[23] In 1973, a particular form of a profit-sharing scheme was introduced. When Handelsbanken met its goal of having a higher return on equity than the average for other listed Swedish banks, a profit share was paid to a foundation named Oktogonen, which kept its fund entirely in Handelsbanken shares. Payment took place only after retirement, which means that all employees were interested in securing the long-term profitability of the bank.[24] Oktogonen owns about 10 per cent of Handelsbanken's shares. The growth in value can only be enjoyed by an employee once he or she reaches the age of sixty. This helps to ensure that employees take a long-term approach as well.[25] Oktogonen is now the largest shareholder in the company. In effect, Handelsbanken has grown its own anchor shareholder![26]

Handelsbanken's story is a reminder to boards and owners that stewardship need not, and must not, be static. It is possible, over time, to change the ownership of the company. It is good stewardship discipline for every board to ask itself once every few years, whether the company's current ownership and business structure is right for its purpose and future plans. The CEO of Tesla, Elon Musk, experienced this in 2018 when he expressed his frustration with his shareholders by suggesting he would take the company private.[27] He very quickly found out that this was prohibitively expensive and impractical. It was an impulsive kick against the constraints of listed status. The issue can be approached from a long-term perspective. There need not be such dramatic change.

There is another lesson to be learnt from the Handelsbanken example. It is about the importance of thinking about the forms of ownership that are most likely to promote the purpose, values and long-term focus of the company.[28] In order to help companies be better stewarded in the future, new hybrid forms of ownership may be the most appropriate, and in an age where employee engagement is crucial to results, expanding ownership by employees is an important element. There is now a growing tendency for owners of family firms to hand over some of the ownership of the business to employees, often in the form of an employee trust.

For example, Cordant, a US$1 billion recruitment company, has decided to change from being a privately-owned family business to a social enterprise.[29] Julian Richer, the founder of Richer Sounds, the UK's largest independent chain of hi-fi and television shops, announced in 2013 that upon his death, the business would be handed over to employees through an employee ownership trust. The plan had been written into his will. He was quoted at the time as saying: "My life's work is my legacy and I haven't got a spoilt child to run the business."[30]

One message stands out from our reflections on the stewardship role of boards. It is that directors are steward leaders, who need to think like owners of the business. In Chapter 6, we will learn that investment institutions are worthy to be described as owners only if they think and behave like stewards.

TOOLKIT — STEWARDSHIP QUESTIONS FOR THE BOARD

1: Setting the course: attention to clarity of purpose, roles and relationships

- How similar are the views of the board and the shareholders about the future of the company's industry and the company's place in it, and what steps are taken to align these views?

- Does the board create opportunities for effective discussion between the board and shareholders about the company's strategy?

- What are the criteria for adapting the company's purpose and role and how have these been developed with input from shareholders?

- What are shareholders' criteria for the board to be effective?

- Is the company clear about the characteristics of the stakeholders it wishes to engage with and the terms on which it will engage with them?

- Do shareholders have opportunities to have effective dialogue with the board?

- Do boards have opportunities to have effective dialogue with the shareholders?

- Are shareholders involved in nominating board members and overseeing remuneration arrangements?

- What mechanisms are there to hold the chairman and board to account for their stewardship? Does the AGM fulfil this purpose?

- How clear are the executive directors about the different duties and responsibilities they have with the company and shareholders as board members and executives?

2: Driving performance: attention to performance and improvement

- How do the board and the shareholders keep abreast of their customers' experience?
- In what ways do the board and shareholders keep their finger on the pulse of the workforce and skill base of the company?
- How does the board review the company's arrangements for dialogue with, and learning from, stakeholders?
- How do the board and the shareholders monitor the culture of and behaviour in the company?
- How does the board keep abreast of risks in the supply chain?
- How are leading indicators built into business strategy, planning and reporting, and over what time horizon?
- How does the board define value beyond just financial metrics?
- Do board and shareholders pay as much attention to the spirit as to the letter of regulations, contracts and obligations?
- What are the board's criteria for changing processes and procedures and how have these been developed with input from shareholders?
- How effective is the management information system at keeping directors and shareholders informed of the company's performance and the changes that need to be made?

3: Part of the landscape: attention to the wider world

- How does the board map the company, its risks and opportunities onto its wider environment?
- How does the board anticipate and deal with potential conflicts among different stakeholders?

- How does the board assess the significance of changes in public policy and the wider environment and the potential impact of these changes on stakeholders?

- What criteria does the board employ for engaging with public policymaking processes and how have these been developed with shareholders?

- What account does the strategy take of the opportunities and risks presented by the company's key relationships?

- How well are the key relationships identified, defined and monitored?

- What dialogue does the board have with shareholders or their representatives on these issues?

- How effectively is the management of the company's relationships reflected in the remuneration and incentive scheme for directors?

4: Planting for the future: coherence over time

- What is the balance between the importance given to short-, medium- and long-term performance indicators?

- Who decides this balance? Does it come from the board or from investor pressures?

- What steps does the board take to ensure that the short-term goals of the company and its shareholders are consistent with the company's long-term strategy?

- Does the board have a clear picture of its shareholders' expectations for the short-, medium- and long-term performance of the company?

- Is the company investing sufficiently in key building blocks, including succession plans, that will sustain long-term performance?

- How effectively are the short-, medium- and long-term objectives of the company reflected in remuneration and incentive schemes?

- Does the company seek out steward investors who share the board's view of the balance between short, medium and long term?

Adapted from *Better stewardship: An agenda for concerted action*, Tomorrow's Company, 2018. Source: http://www.tomorrowscompany.com/up-content/uploads/2018/01/Better-Stewardship-An-agenda-for-concerted-action_-25Jan2018.pdf

Box 7: Stewardship questions for the board

TOOLKIT — THE BOARD MANDATE
An agenda for the board's discussion

Who are we and what do we stand for?

- What is special and distinctive about us — our 'essence' that defines us? (i.e. not something that could be said about any of our peers)

- What is the primary purpose of this company?

- To whom do we believe we owe our prime responsibility?

What values, reputation and culture do we want?

- What are the core values to which we aspire? Can we prioritise them?

- How do these translate into actions?

- How do we define the culture of the company?

- Are the value drivers embedded into the culture of the company?

- What are the issues on which we won't negotiate/compromise — and does this mean that we would turn down the opportunity for short-term success? What are our lines in the sand?

- Are our policies and products/services aligned with our values? How do we ensure this continues?

- What is our approach to diversity? How do we actively encourage this?

How do we create a successful, sustainable organisation?

- What is our core business model? What are our main products/services? How do we make money from them?

- Can we describe our value chain?

- What is our approach to our value chain? Which parts of the value chain do we focus on?

- What are the characteristics of the markets in which we operate?

- What is it about us, in terms of our competences, and product/service offerings, which make these markets a good fit?

- Do we consciously use this knowledge to judge whether to enter new markets?

- What are our core criteria that must be met before we will enter a new market?

- What is our approach to sustainability? In what way do we aim to add value to the society or societies in which we operate?

- Have sustainability issues relevant to the business of the company been identified, and are they incorporated into our long-term strategy? Does the board know whether there is buy-in to the strategy from the top to the bottom in the company?

- Do we make an honest assessment of how we remove value from society? And what is our approach in dealing with the "downside"?

How do we develop our business?

- What is our approach to renewal and/or growth?

- What is our approach to talent? How do we inspire and engage our people? Do we seek to grow talent predominantly from within?

- How do we create and preserve our corporate memory so that we learn from mistakes effectively?

- How do we generate and discuss options and turn the best into concrete actions?

- What are the key criteria by which we make decisions?

- What does our future blueprint look like?

What is our appetite for risk?

- What are the five major challenges and/or opportunities that could make or break our company?

- What is our distinctive approach to risk and opportunity across the business compared to our peers and competitors?

- In which areas do we seek to be a leader and/or undertake innovative risky ventures and where are we content to be just the average in our industry?

- What technological, social and political changes and discontinuities might we face?

What relationships do we have with our stakeholders?

- Who are the major stakeholder groupings linked to the company? And how do we balance the needs of different stakeholders?

- What are the needs, interests and expectations of these stakeholder groups?

- Are our objectives in harmony with the concerns of our employees and customers?

- Does management have an interactive relationship with these stakeholder groupings? Is the relationship proactive or reactive?

- What is our fundamental approach to our relationships with immediate suppliers/customers? Are we committed to ensuring our suppliers have the same standards that we do and how do we monitor that?

Note: A mandate is not a mission statement. It is a living statement for and by the board, continually refreshed and reinforced through the leadership of the chairman, actively engaging with all of the members of the board. If each member of the board can describe what is distinctive about the company in broadly the same way, the mandate would have been successfully embedded.

Adapted from *Better stewardship: An agenda for concerted action*, Tomorrow's Company, 2018. Source: http://www.tomorrowscompany.com/up-content/uploads/2018/01/Better-Stewardship-An-agenda-for-concerted-action_-25Jan2018.pdf

Box 8: The board mandate

Chapter 6

Institutional Investors as Stewards

Below is an advertisement for a position of investment analyst that was posted by a recruitment company in London:

> An enthusiastic, energetic and hardworking investment analyst who has a successful and consistent track record of achieving high returns for clients. Possessing extensive knowledge of global financial markets, including a wide variety of industries and sectors. Employing an evidence-based approach to all projects and experienced in assisting senior analysts and fund managers in writing accurate company-specific reports. Currently looking for a suitable position with an exciting and expanding company.[1]

Analysts, like those sought in the advertisement, research and review companies listed on stock exchanges. They, like their counterparts all over the world, provide analysis to guide investors on their choice of stocks. It is interesting to look at some of the qualifications sought for this role. While knowledge of *financial markets* is specified, experience or understanding of actual companies, their leadership and governance, and what drives long-term value for shareholders, is not mentioned at all. In other words, any knowledge of what it takes to be enduring and successful, or any kind of expertise on whether a company is a steward or not, is not emphasised. If a food expert is expected to know something about nutrition before advising consumers on what they should eat, why is understanding wealth creation not a necessity for the job scope of an investment analyst? Wealth is created in companies. Why then is the process of investment analysis so remote from the stewardship experience of wealth creation?

Rebalancing Capital Markets

The answer lies in the tension that will always exist in capital markets between owning and trading shares. There is nothing wrong with having a part of the capital markets that thrives on buying and selling company stocks. This creates the liquidity that allows other investors to come in and out of the market when they need to. But, as the world discovered in 2008 and many times before that, there is a price to pay when balance is lost and fundamentals of responsible wealth creation go out of the window. Not only do innocent savers get hit in the process as the market crashes, more significantly, the relentless pressure on companies to maximise earnings changes the behaviour of people working in listed firms and drives them away from stewardship behaviour. Enron is a good example of a company that took the pressure to perform financially too far.

Stock markets which came into existence to provide primary capital for companies have also changed their nature. They initially started as mutual organisations which existed to serve their members, the customers. Today, they are listed companies which are themselves striving to maximise earnings. Their main purpose now is to promote the trading of stocks for profit. Often, more money is made by stock turnover, promoting day trading and rapid stock volatility. Much of the research generated by analysts is used to fuel that trading. It is estimated that half of the market barely moves at all, 30 per cent of the market trades infrequently, and the remaining 20 per cent of stocks are being traded actively.

However, contrary to assumptions, such a way of doing business does not always generate the most profit. A study by McKinsey Global Institute demonstrated that firms focusing their business on the long term had 47 per cent higher revenue and 36 per cent greater earnings over a period of fourteen years between 2001 and 2014.[2]

The stewardship imperative in listed companies is, therefore, not to eliminate trading or even try to stop speculation on share prices. It is to strengthen the part of the market that is concerned with the protection and enhancement of value through effective ownership so that the trading side of capital markets is not allowed to impinge on or overwhelm the stewardship side. There are serious weaknesses in the way our current system of investment in companies works.

So far, this book has described the role of leaders and boards in addressing these weaknesses as they seek to promote the long-term success of their companies. Now, it is time to travel further upstream, by focusing on the agenda for those who represent the ultimate clients and beneficiaries in their role as asset owners and asset managers.

Asset managers, otherwise described as portfolio or fund managers, do not or at least should not exist to serve themselves. They are entrusted with assets and resources by the individual savers, investors and asset owners — pension funds, insurance companies and investment funds. It should be noted that asset owners, too, have influence over the companies in which they invest. Stewardship is the thread that is needed to connect everyone in the system —

individuals and those who give those individuals advice, pension trustees, insurance companies, fund managers, advisers, as well as the regulators and lawmakers who set the rules.

Chairmen and CEOs often complain that in meetings with analysts, they are seldom asked questions about the company's purpose and values, their people and the culture of the organisation, let alone their relationships with suppliers and communities. There is no doubt that the pressure to create quick returns in capital markets affects the behaviour of people leading companies. It tends to shorten their time horizons. This in turn has an impact on the health of an economy or society as it depends on these companies to create wealth and provide employment. There is some research to support the concern that this pressure changes behaviour and undermines the stewardship of companies. A 2005 survey of 401 financial executives by John Graham and Campbell R. Harvey of Duke University and Shivaram Rajgopal of the University of Washington found that 80 per cent of respondents said they would decrease value-creating spending on research and development, advertising, maintenance, and hiring in order to meet earnings benchmarks. The authors suggest that this preoccupation with reported earnings at the expense of value creation is linked to a desire to influence stock prices, the respondents' own careers and reputations.[3]

There are some forces for change which are working in the other direction. Foremost among these, ironically, has been the growth of indexed funds or so-called passive investing. A fund manager whose funds are invested in an index is freed from concerns about whether the share price is going to go up or down. Such a fund manager cannot sell the stock and is limited to selecting the index and trying to influence the stocks in the index to go up. Index investment is very competitive and is marketed on the basis of its lower costs. This means that the index fund management company may be tempted not to invest too much in the exercise of stewardship.

BlackRock, the largest institutional investor in the world and also a leader in indexed funds is leading the way to better stewardship. Its CEO Larry Fink, in his 2019 letter urging business leaders to steward their companies in the right direction in the current polarised climate, reminded them that:

> Purpose is not a mere tagline or marketing campaign; it is a company's fundamental reason for being — what it does every day to create value for its stakeholders. Purpose is not the sole pursuit of profits but the animating force for achieving them. Profits are in no way inconsistent with purpose — in fact, profits and purpose are inextricably linked. Profits are essential if a company is to effectively serve all of its stakeholders over time —not only shareholders, but also employees, customers, and communities. Similarly, when a company truly understands and expresses its purpose, it functions with the focus and strategic discipline that drive long-term profitability. Purpose unifies management, employees and communities. It drives ethical behaviour and creates an essential check on actions that go against the best interests of stakeholders. Purpose guides culture, provides a framework for consistent decision-making, and, ultimately, helps sustain long-term financial returns for the shareholders of your company.

Communicating with the CEOs of companies, of which Black-Rock is a part owner, in very much the tone that one might expect a family business owner briefing a new CEO on the importance of stewardship, Fink said:

> As a CEO myself, I feel first-hand the pressures com-
> panies face in today's polarized environment and the
> challenges of navigating them. Stakeholders are pushing
> companies to wade into sensitive social and political
> issues — especially as they see governments failing to
> do so effectively. As CEOs, we don't always get it right.
> And what is appropriate for one company may not be
> for another. One thing, however, is certain: the world
> needs your leadership. As divisions continue to deepen,
> companies must demonstrate their commitment to the
> countries, regions, and communities where they oper-
> ate, particularly on issues central to the world's future
> prosperity. Companies cannot solve every issue of public
> importance, but there are many — from retirement
> to infrastructure to preparing workers for the jobs of
> the future — that cannot be solved without corporate
> leadership.[4]

So here is the head of one of the world's largest investment companies asserting the vital importance of stewardship. If that spirit could genuinely be spread among asset owners, asset managers and those who advise and provide research for them, there would indeed be a chance that more listed companies might rediscover the human purposes of business and move towards a stewardship view. The agenda is already defined for stewardship investment.

BlackRock was one of six institutional investors which came together after the global financial crisis to develop their vision and agenda in a report. The resultant *2020 Stewardship — Improving the quality of investor stewardship*, which was published in 2012, highlighted the need for a "critical mass of investor stewards".[5] The report also acknowledged that "not every shareholder can or needs to be a good steward" and identified the key challenges. These challenges were about both the quality and quantity of stewardship. The six institutions argued that "for the sake of beneficiaries and companies, we need to build a critical mass of stewardship investors — funds which are capable of engaging companies in constructive dialogue and holding their boards accountable to shareowners".[6]

Since the launch of the UK Stewardship Code in 2010, other countries, including Singapore, have come up with various versions of and approaches to stewardship codes and principles for institutional investors. The ICGN Model Mandate initiative, referred to in Chapter 4, is another example of collaborative work among steward investors.

There are many professionals in the investment industry who are working to weave stewardship into the investment chain so that, over time, it becomes a stewardship value chain. There is a clear agenda for those occupying each link in the chain. Before describing this agenda, however, it is first worth considering two other related issues. The first of these is the relationship between stewardship and ESG. The second is the impact of shareholder activism and takeover bids on stewardship.

STEWARDSHIP AND ESG

The Principles for Responsible Investment (PRI) is a global organisation formed by institutional investors committed to six principles of responsible investment. PRI defines responsible investment as:

> An approach to investing that aims to incorporate
> environmental, social and governance (ESG) factors
> into investment decisions, to better manage risk and
> generate sustainable, long-term returns.[7]

ESG criteria are, therefore, tests that responsible investors
use to screen potential investments. Environmental criteria test
how a company performs in its impact on nature. Social criteria
are concerned with how a company manages relationships with
its employees, suppliers, customers and the communities where
it operates. Governance criteria deal with a company's formal
decision-making processes, board structure, director accountability,
executive and non-executive appointments, as well as detailed issues
like executive pay, audits, internal controls and shareholder rights.

Notice what ESG does not generally cover. It is not concerned
with the character of a company. It does not cover assessments of the
way a company is led. It does not involve any attempt to understand
the uniqueness or personality of the company, from its founding
onwards. Every company is different, and what ESG does well is to
bring to bear some universal expectations about the company, its
impact and behaviour. What the language of ESG lacks is the kind
of integrated approach to the definition of value that was described
in Chapter 4 on fiduciary duty.

Stewardship, on the other hand, is concerned with the
uniqueness, character, history and personality of the business.
A good steward of a business has a closer relationship with that
business and an overall sense of its human purpose. Through this,
he or she has a holistic view of the value that the business is intended
to create. Stewardship treads where generalised criteria of responsible
business and investment dare not. ESG is looking from the outside

in. Stewardship is looking from the inside out. ESG reaches its limits where stewardship really starts.

SHAREHOLDER ACTIVISM AND STEWARDSHIP: TALE OF TWO TAKEOVERS

There will always be a part of the market that exists to strip assets, to find a company where there is an easy opportunity to cut overheads, boost immediate profits, push up the share price, and then sell. That is what some hedge funds exist to do. And hedge funds have their place in the ecosystem of capital markets. The market needs buyers as well as sellers. Indeed, just as there are natural predators in the food chain, so it is natural that there are predators in capital markets. The danger is when predators get out of control and nature's balance is destroyed. When capital markets lose too much ground to predators, both wealth creation and society will be the casualties.

It is tough but not impossible to maintain a sense of good stewardship in a listed company with dispersed shareholding. The CEO may want to be bold and set out a principled approach. But there are analysts, journalists and critics among the investor group just waiting for the first slip-up, the first sign that they have "lost their grip", "taken their eye off the ball" or "gone soft".

This is not to mention the much higher burden of reporting and regulation that goes with being a listed company. CEOs and finance directors often have to travel across continents, giving the same presentations many times a day in the name of reporting and regulation.

To compound the difficulty of being a listed company, there is the lurking threat of takeover. On some occasions, the drive for corporate control can be healthy. It is a form of sanction that can be used to replace a sleepy management and put an underperforming business in better hands. On other occasions, however, it can be a means by which a board which has been investing for the long term is undermined and pressured into abandoning the company's long-held stewardship precepts to the whims of the market. This process is actively encouraged by investment banks which have no interest in long-term wealth creation, and can earn large fees for making deals happen without risking any downside if the deals later turn out to be value-destroying for the company in question.

Cadbury: The story of a hostile takeover

Consider the contrasting fortunes of two well-known companies in the food industry, both confronted in recent years by an aggressive attack from the outside — Cadbury and Olam.

Cadbury, based in the UK, is a British global producer of confectionery. It was founded in 1824 in Bourneville, UK. Its founders were Quakers, a non-conformist religious order. Quaker capitalists believed that the goal of business was to serve society and improve local communities, rather than simply acquire wealth. As historian and family member Deborah Cadbury puts it:

> They were trying to come up with something that they thought would be a nutritious alternative to alcohol, which was the ruin of many poor families. They were trying to come up with a business idea that was actually going to help people, and cocoa was this amazing new commodity and they thought they could make a business out of this nutritious drink.[8]

Cadbury also had a strong commitment to improving the pay and health of employees, as well as the education and housing opportunities for them, believing that this was right and would benefit the business. It introduced Saturdays off, pensions, unemployment and sickness benefits "and even free doctors, free dentists and vitamin pills for staff".[9] Before merging with Kraft, Cadbury was listed on the London Stock Exchange. The company had grown through mergers and de-mergers and had at that time embarked on a strategy that was just beginning to show results.

Nevertheless, Cadbury was bought out by the US firm Kraft in January 2010. Mentioned in Chapter 5, in 2008, Kraft was the world's second-largest food company, with a revenue of over US$33.6 billion and employing 98,000 people. When Kraft made a bid, unlike the case of Unilever, Cadbury went in a separate direction.

Once a bid was made, the board of Cadbury had a choice. In principle, a board of directors, which felt that the Cadbury approach to business was worth preserving and which disliked the very different business culture of Kraft, could and should have rejected the bid on the grounds of stewardship and suitability, not price. As was pointed out to them at the time, they owed their duty to the company, and had to decide whether ownership by Kraft was best for the future prospects of Cadbury.[10] But this was easier said than done. The Cadbury board was under intense pressure from the shareholders, nearly half of whom were in the US. It would have needed the cornerstone support of loyal institutional investors who had faith in the leadership of the company and its longer-term prospects. Only 5 per cent of its shares were owned by short-term traders at the time of the Kraft bid, but many of the pension funds and fund managers who might have supported the board chose to take their profits. Hedge funds owned a third of the shares by the time the takeover was sealed.

Only time will tell whether the new owners will be good stewards of Cadbury's assets and preserve and renew its unique culture. After almost a decade, the signs are not encouraging. For example, the company has abandoned its membership of the Fairtrade Foundation through which manufacturers agree to pay an ethically acceptable minimum price for cocoa from growers in Africa. It closed a plant in the UK which it had promised investors and employees it would keep open. The company score as measured by YouGov's BrandIndex, which measures quality and customer perception of the brand, has slipped from forty-three to about twenty-five in the six years since the takeover.[11] This is not surprising given its parent company's poor performance. As mentioned in Chapter 5, Kraft merged with H.J. Heinz in 2015 but suffers from a host of ills often associated with relentless cost-cutting.[12]

It cannot be assumed that Cadbury would have thrived in its previous form as a listed company. However, what this example shows is that under the approach taken by today's investment institutions, any publicly listed company with dispersed shareholding is vulnerable to takeover bids. Unlike family businesses or businesses with an anchor shareholder, Cadbury's board and management were not in a position to protect its unique company culture. Perhaps the Cadbury board could have prevented this disaster if it had chosen a hybrid form of listing, following the examples of Handelsbanken or that of the Tatas, which were described in the previous chapter, rather than ceding control altogether. And perhaps the institutions which sold their shares during the bid process would have made different decisions if they had asked their ultimate clients and beneficiaries if they wished to put an end to the stewardship of Cadbury.

Olam: Anchored to success

Compare Cadbury with the example of Olam. Olam is also a company in the food industry. It was established in 1989 in Nigeria. Today, it is a multi-product, multinational agri-business with 70,000 employees. It has established sourcing and marketing operations in Indonesia, Laos, Vietnam, Thailand, China, Papua New Guinea, the Middle East, Central Asia, and Brazil. It has in the past faced challenges from non-governmental organisations such as Mighty Earth for its palm oil sourcing and production processes. However, Olam has since made practical efforts to address these criticisms and has reinvented itself as a company that strives for sustainability.

Olam's business began with the export of cashews from Nigeria and then expanded into exports of cotton, cocoa and peanuts, also from Nigeria. It was originally headquartered in London but then relocated to Singapore in 1996. It filed an Initial Public Offering in 2005, listing on the Singapore Stock Exchange. However, unlike Cadbury, it had a small number of significant anchor shareholders, one of which was Temasek Holdings. Muddy Waters sought to undermine Olam by publishing a critical research report making allegations about its accounting standards and short-selling its shares, thus, rendering it at risk of a hostile takeover.[13] But one of Olam's anchor shareholders, Temasek, believed in the management of the company. It offered to buy the shares of any shareholder tempted to accept the takeover bid from Muddy Waters. As a result, the bid failed and the company was saved from being broken apart. It has since continued from strength to strength.

So, although it is possible for a company to be well-stewarded while exposing some of its share register to public markets, it is impossible for this stewardship to be sustained if all its shares are for sale and the company can be taken over at any time. An excellent company can build up its stock of culture, heritage, traditions of service and loyalty and even sacrifice, and still be taken over by new owners who place no value on these intangibles. A predator company will only likely focus on ways to increase short-term profits by cutting costs.

Hedge funds will buy the shares at a premium and tempt longer-term shareholders to sell. Other previously more passive institutional investors may be unable to resist this temptation even if they are supportive of the current management, as selling will allow them to make a speculative gain on the portfolio. There is a tangible reward for that while there is no equivalent immediate reward for staying loyal to a management you believe in. Asset managers also tend to be rewarded in the short term and are likely to get a better bonus if they record a windfall gain. Unless the ultimate shareholders have given clear instructions that shares are not to be sold to hostile bidders, these fund managers may act like agents, concentrating solely on financial returns in the short term instead of the creation of longer-term value. It is only when the longer-term institutions are loyal and responsible that they will hold out and act more like stewards.

This is the ultimate inherent weakness of a dispersed-ownership listed company. Will institutions which claim to be good stewards show loyalty to companies like Cadbury and Olam? Stewardship matters, but we have a long way to go before its importance is recognised throughout the value chain that connects savers and beneficiaries to crucial institutional decisions about opportunistic acquisitions. For this reason, all listed company boards need to think hard about these risks to prepare long before danger arrives. They need to look at their current business model and consider the merits of having an anchor (steward) shareholder or a hybrid business form, like that of Tata or Handelsbanken, which gives it more control over the company's destiny.[14]

This tale of two takeovers also leaves questions for asset owners and asset managers to answer. The ultimate defence against shareholder opportunism is to use the same mandate process to force the intermediaries who put investor capital behind such approaches to check whether it is actually what the ultimate clients and beneficiaries want done with their money. The requirement under corporate governance and stewardship codes for boards to conduct their own mandate process would, where fund management companies, pension funds and insurance firms are concerned, help bring these issues into the open.

STEWARDSHIP INVESTMENT: THE AGENDA

Individuals

We want to see a world in which ordinary consumers are able to opt for and encourage stewardship when buying suitable financial products. It has always been important for investors to understand where their money is invested and how it is being put to work. Now that more and more individuals are buying their own pensions and making their own savings arrangements, such knowledge is even more pertinent. They need to be offered simple choices which enable them to exercise influence over the investment funds and ultimately, the companies which are investing their wealth. Financial services companies will be more likely to offer this choice if individuals start showing that they care that the fund managers who work for them vigilantly observe the companies in which their money is invested. A toolkit comprising questions for financial advisers, pension funds and even individual savers to ask fund managers is as follows:

- What is your stance on the concepts of stewardship?

- Are you playing your part in ensuring that the companies you invest individuals' money in are well-stewarded? Which of the funds that you offer or recommend take stewardship seriously? Have you thought about reducing the number of companies in the portfolio so that you can do a better job of stewardship?

- How often will you talk to the companies you invest in? How do you plan to find out what really goes on within the company? How do you know they are ethical and responsible? How do you tell whether they are well-run? How do you know that they develop talent and adapt to the changing marketplace? How do you make sure the management thinks long-term and is not just driving up the share price to fatten their immediate bonuses?

Trustees of pension funds

In countries where there are investors' Stewardship Codes or Principles, the fund manager which is a signatory to these documents is required to make clear its policy on stewardship. Pension funds need to play their part in holding fund managers to account for their stewardship policies. In support of the concerns expressed above, the trustees should ask themselves:

- Does our statement of investment principles ensure that our assets are managed on our behalf with a proper degree of stewardship?

- What proportion of our total portfolio is prudent and realistic enough to operate under a stewardship mandate? What criteria, if any, do we set for intervention by some or all of our fund managers in particular situations e.g. our approach to proposed takeovers, director remuneration and disclosures by companies around short- or longer-term risks, ethical behaviour, health, safety, carbon and water usage?

- Do we apply these concerns to listed companies alone or to our investments in private equity, infrastructure, property and other asset classes?

- Having clarified our approach to stewardship in our statement of investment principles, have we adequately reflected this in the investment mandates that we have issued, and in the way that they define and review investment performance?

- Should we start to instruct our investment consultants to move towards issuing longer-term mandates to fund managers?

In the words of Judge Mervyn King, Chair Emeritus of the International Integrated Reporting Council and the Chairman Emeritus of the Global Reporting Initiative:

> There is absolutely no doubt that institutional investors, such as the trustees of pension funds, have an onerous duty, I believe even more onerous than a director. They are making decisions which will impact people's lives 30 to 40 years hence, and they must assess the quality of governance, of management, and all these so-called non-financial aspects which make up the economic value of a company, before investing your and my money in a company.[15]

Investment consultants who advise pension funds

Because the job of the pension trustee is so complex, trustees may not be able to exercise and express what they mean by stewardship, and will leave it to the experts, that is, the investment consultants. A toolkit for investment consultants could be as follows:

- Where do you stand on stewardship? What is your definition of stewardship? What are you doing to encourage your clients, your competitors and others in the system to take stewardship seriously? What measures do you take to ensure you are a steward leader instead of simply reacting to pressure?

- What criteria do you use to assess the stewardship exercised by different fund managers?

- Do you agree that stewardship is about a great deal more than ensuring that fund managers cast votes at the Annual General Meeting (AGM)? What do you look at when assessing the quality of dialogue and engagement that fund managers have with companies?

- What is your understanding about the role that stewardship can play in the fulfilment of the fiduciary obligations of pension funds? What advice do you give to pension trustees about the relationship between fiduciary duty and stewardship?

- What are you doing to inform trustees about the quality of stewardship demonstrated by competing fund managers, and equip them with the ability to issue stewardship mandates and select the fund managers who are best equipped to fulfil such mandates?

- What are you doing to encourage your clients to come up with a clear policy on stewardship?

- What are you doing to work with other investment consultants, as well as the pension fund and fund management industry to build a clear set of stewardship criteria?

Fund management companies and fund managers

Fund management companies exist to create value for their clients and to fulfil the terms of the mandate that is given to them. They have many different approaches to this end and not all of them exercise stewardship. Some are simply traders of shares. But other funds, which have shares in listed or unlisted companies, in property and other investment assets, have the opportunity and the responsibility to be stewards. Each fund owes it to clients and potential clients to explain what it is doing about stewardship. This includes index funds, which hold the shares of a company as long as it remains in the index, and therefore have ample opportunity to influence those companies.

Individually, one or two fund managers may, for a few periods, beat the index. But in the end, what helps clients most is a healthy company sector over which stewardship is being exercised. It is important to note that stewardship must be practised and thought of holistically. Fund managers who think only of the effect that good stewardship has over the companies currently in their own portfolio are not seeing the whole picture. Ultimately, clients' wealth improves in tandem with the performance of a much wider group of companies as a whole. Good stewardship is about the health of the whole forest, not just that of a few chosen trees within it. Hence, to be able to have checks on their fund managers, clients and beneficiaries need to know their approach at three levels.

Firstly, the approach of the fund management institution

as a whole. Secondly, the approach of each individual fund that operates within that house. And thirdly, the extent to which either collaborates with other fund managers or institutions. A toolkit of questions to ask at the level of the fund management institution is as follows:

- What do you mean by stewardship? Overall, would you describe yourself as an investor who practises the five stewardship concepts (see chapter 2)?

- How many of the individual funds within your control could reasonably be defined as steward investors? Have you categorised each of them in any way which helps clients choose between funds on the basis of their stewardship content?

- Do you have index funds (where your holdings are permanent as long as the company stays in the index) and what do you do, on your own or in partnership with others, to hold these companies accountable?

At the level of each individual fund, a toolkit of questions to ask may include:

- Which of the following steps are you taking to promote the spread of stewardship?

  1. Consistently and thoughtfully voting at AGMs. By thoughtfully, we mean: If you are outsourcing the voting, have you set your own clear stewardship policy which your proxy organisation can follow? Are there circumstances where you or your proxy agency will adjust their vote as a result of dialogue with the company?

  2. Are you engaging with companies on strategy, risk, environmental, ethical, social and governance issues, including

the performance and evaluation of board members, and the current or future composition of the board?

3. Are you a signatory to the Code or Principles of Responsible Investment? Are you integrating responsible investment concerns with those of risk and future performance, as recommended, by introducing greater stewardship skills into your engagement teams so that they are equipped to discuss the range of issues listed previously?

4. In light of recent research showing that most fund managers have larger portfolios than they need to hold from a risk perspective, have you defined how far portfolio size can be reduced in the interest of closer attention to companies in the portfolio?[16] Or have you defined a programme of collaboration with other investors that allows you to achieve the same focus with shared stewardship effort?

Life insurance companies

Insurance companies collect savings and life insurance premiums from many savers and clients, and we expect them to be good stewards of our investments. We expect boards of insurance companies to provide answers to the following questions:

- What do you mean by stewardship? Overall, would you describe yourself as a steward investor? What do you do, on your own or in partnership with others, to achieve what you mean by stewardship?

- What is the body which is clearly and separately responsible for setting the stewardship policy of the investment fund which invests assets on behalf of life policyholders? How is this stewardship policy communicated to policyholders?

- How does this body monitor the stewardship exercised on its behalf by fund managers? How do the fund managers give an account of their stewardship? How are the results of this process communicated to their policyholders?

- How many of the individual funds within your control could reasonably be defined as steward investors? Or are there any other ways which help clients choose between funds on the basis of their stewardship content? With your index funds, what do you do, on your own or in partnership with others, to hold companies accountable and stimulate their performance?

FOR ALL ASSET OWNERS AND ASSET MANAGERS

Developing a clear mandate with the board

Shareholders and owners elect the board and it is vital that the board defines its mandate. In their engagement with companies, fund managers will naturally ask the board if it has been through a process of defining its own mandate. This then provides a valuable cue for discussions about the key stewardship action areas — clarity of purpose, time horizon, discussions about the external environment of the company and how to ensure continual improvement in its performance.

It paves the way for directors to be challenged more effectively and constructively on a company's current performance and future prospects. The result is that company management will be encouraged to pay less attention to short-term fluctuations in the share price and instead engage investors in understanding and assessing key business processes. Once the mandate is in place, there is then the opportunity for continued dialogue between the board and steward investors around these issues. This should then take priority over much of the current investor relations activities. In their engagement with the company, asset managers will ask:

- How far have you as a board discussed and defined your mandate? Is the company setting out its purpose, values and strategy in a way that opens up proper discussion about the long-term as well as the short-term prospects and progress of the company?

- Does this mandate form the basis of your long-term communications with your investors and defence against opportunistic takeovers or manipulation by a minority of investors?

Engaging with the company and its board

If there is one single question a fund manager could ask a Chairman or a CEO during an engagement, what would it be? This was a question asked of a fund manager on a panel at an international forum on stewarding investment. It was disappointing, to say the least, when the response was, "I always ask the Chairman or CEO: when was the last time you looked at your company's share price?" Not only does it seem shallow and short-term in nature to expect a CEO to be so pre-occupied with the current share price, it begs a further question about the fund manager's motivation and what direction the follow-on dialogue would take. With engagement with the Chairman or CEO of portfolio companies now specifically encouraged by established Stewardship Codes and Principles in many countries, investors are squandering the opportunity for fostering stewardship if they focus on the act rather than the intent of engagement. Questions to the Chairman or CEO ought to go beyond what is already available in reports or from briefings by the company's finance or investor relations employees. Engagement with the Chairman or the CEO could, and ought to, include matters related to value creation, success and the stewardship concepts — ownership, purpose, having a long-term view, relationships and community. For instance, it could begin with "how does your company go about creating value?" This question would bring about an answer which could shed light on whether the company has been thinking through what its success would look like. The answer would likely relate much to the company's purpose and values. It does not reduce everything to one, inevitably incomplete, measure such as profit before tax, cash flow, earnings per share or share price. Such a question acknowledges the uniqueness of each business and gives a company scope to design its own framework or measure of success.

The stewardship agenda has implications for society, shareholders, the board, and the management of companies. Without effective stewardship, society will not get the robust, principled companies it needs. Without stewardship, it is impossible to sustain good corporate governance or corporate social responsibility. And without it, economies may find themselves oscillating continually between rampant greed and rigid regulation. The role of institutional investors and their clients is crucial. As the investment value chain becomes increasingly complex and indirect, it is all the more relevant and important that each investment participant is infused with the spirit of stewardship. For the value chain to work well owners need to have a stewardship mentality. That is the key to turning the investment value chain into a stewardship value chain, with stewardship as the thread running through, from the ultimate savers and beneficiaries to the investment intermediaries who interact with the board and management of portfolio companies.

Regulators, too, have a role in laying the foundations for effective stewardship. They can strengthen the rules and incentives within which investment institutions and company directors and executives will operate. Moreover, the state, besides being a lawmaker and regulator has multiple opportunities to create the right climate for responsible wealth creation, not least through its direct role as an asset owner, asset manager and investor. The state as steward is the subject of the next chapter.

Chapter 7

The State as Steward

Governments do not have the option. They are stewards by nature. Governments, in general, would readily acknowledge their obligation "to be wholehearted and responsible in their management of the assets with which they have been entrusted so that they pass them on in a better condition". This is the very definition of stewardship. The approach that the state takes towards wealth creation will, however, be a particularly vital determinant of its overall success. In economies around the world, in different forms and varying degrees, the role of the state in promoting responsible wealth creation with an emphasis on the long term is crucial.

Governments' stewardship influences over wealth creation can be both direct and indirect. Directly, with respect to the market, the state acts as an investor, asset owner, asset manager, client and customer. In these capacities, it can have a direct impact on the operation of the companies and the investment institutions that it owns, manages or does business with.

Indirectly, the state has the opportunity to be a facilitator of responsible wealth creation, influencing the economic environment and business landscape through making the rules and setting the rewards and penalties via regulation. It sets the tone and lays the foundation for responsible wealth creation through incentives and policy initiatives, and crucially, through leadership by example.

In Chapter 4, markets and the structure of law and regulation were described as the hardware of wealth creation. Stewardship behaviours are the software — ways of working that, if pursued throughout the system, can deliver results which lead to a better capitalism.

In the first half of this chapter, we describe the government's direct role in the market. In the second half, we consider how the government can promote a climate of stewardship using the hardware of law, regulation and policies, as well as through leadership by example. But first, we consider responsible wealth creation and the priority areas from the perspective of the state.

Responsible Wealth Creation

In many parts of the world, there is dissatisfaction with large-scale businesses. Big companies are often perceived by the general public as faceless, uncaring organisations, doing deals and benefitting people at the top while squeezing every last drop of effort from those at the bottom of the social hierarchy. Such perceptions may have taken the emphasis away from the solid core of businesses which consistently nurture relationships and have a sense of purpose beyond profit.

Meanwhile, in many jurisdictions around the world, entrepreneurs from businesses of various industries may be frustrated by the shifts and increase in regulations and government policies. It is difficult for governments to find the right balance when attempting to satisfy many diverse needs, as there will always be competing demands among customers, employees, shareholders and citizens. However, it is reasonable to expect that governments should think holistically about the issues and develop a coherent approach to tackle them, as well as focus on long-term wealth creation for all.

The public can lose confidence in the system of wealth creation when businesses do not create value in a responsible manner. For instance, there are stories about CEOs continuing to receive a high salary or resigning with severance packages running into the millions amid business collapse, plant closures, job losses and takeovers. This is made worse in some countries by scandals related to corruption or embezzlement of company funds by top managers. As a result, there is usually mounting pressure for governments to take ever stricter action to regulate businesses. This often creates a vicious circle. In some countries, that can mean more interference in markets, resulting in changes to regulations that make it harder for businesses to plan and operate, let alone innovate. Overall, this leads to further loss of trust in government measures.

It is always easier for governments to tackle the symptoms and symbolic causes of such mistrust than the underlying reason, which is that the wealth-creation process is not felt to be serving the human purposes of business. Although many governments understand the problem, few think and act systemically to solve it, and many may not have the will and stability to do so. They may legislate to strengthen trade union representation, extend corporate reporting requirements, increase governance, limit overseas takeovers or take sections of business activity more directly under government jurisdiction. As part of a coherent approach and with consistent implementation, such policy changes can help to improve things. The danger is that, if done in isolation, such changes merely add to the list of restrictions and bureaucratic obligations and get in the way of innovation. They may unwittingly create the trappings of a solution and engender compliance, but do they solve the problems?

Enter stewardship, a philosophy and a way of doing and investing in business that focuses on human purposes. Governments which truly wish to stimulate trustworthy wealth creation will need to see themselves as stewards, with a solemn responsibility to take care of the wealth-creation system that they are entrusted with, and to see things long term, so as to pass assets on to their successors in a better condition. Governments need to work in a consistent way on both the hardware and the software — the rules and, more subtly, the behaviours and attitudes.

There are two kinds of pressure that can help ensure business activities are channelled towards value creation and away from short-term vested financial success. One is the stewardship influence of the shareholders and the boards they elect to direct the company. Governments can have influence over the investment value chain as an owner, investor and asset manager.

The other type of pressure comes from the policies, rules and incentives that governments create and put in place, as well as the behaviour that they demonstrate, influencing others to follow. The best outcomes are achieved when both types of pressure work in support of each other. The goal is to have a market that is, and is seen to be, free and fair. This could be carefully nurtured by the joint efforts of the government, investors and business organisations, and by the influence from their stakeholders, such that businesses can operate in ways that create value responsibly. Companies faced with these two types of pressure can be helped by a third — a strong supply of information which allows individuals, when acting as consumers, employees or investors, to give due preference to those who are contributing the most value to society. The supply of information can also help individuals sieve out companies that are out for a quick buck at the expense of society, as well as those which are failing in their stewardship obligations.

What are the priorities of the state? In Chapter 5, we described the four stewardship priorities for any board. These priority areas which form the basis of good corporate governance also hold good for governments. Like boards of companies and institutional investors, governments can focus on the four practical priorities of stewardship to guide their own efforts in managing state assets and handing them over to their successors in a better shape than they inherited them.

The Four Priority Areas Applicable to The Role Of The State as Steward

First, to achieve clarity

As with boards and investors, governments need to be clear about their view on their role as steward, and their values. They need to spell out their approach to wealth creation. They also need to define the underlying philosophy that guides their policymaking across a wide range of areas, not just employment law, trade policy and regulation. Governments and leaders may come and go, but there has to be an underlying consistency that makes longer-term planning and investment worthwhile. A comprehensive policy for wealth creation would embrace the way people are educated and equipped with the skills that tomorrow's enterprises may need. Governments should map out the stewardship value chain and regulate its activities in a systematic way. They should ensure that different departmental policies align in creating a coherent climate for the longer term, fostering responsible and sustainable wealth creation that meets the needs of the current generation without compromising those of the next.

Second, to encourage continual improvement

The state should seek to progressively enhance its wealth-creating capacity. It sets objectives in all the key areas and tests the country's success against them. A balanced scorecard for a country or region would measure progress on the things that matter most, beyond the short term. Conventional indicators like capital formation, productivity and gross domestic product (GDP) growth are parts of this scorecard but other indicators are needed. These may include literacy and skill levels, availability of training and retraining opportunities for those facing economic disruption, child development, environmental sustainability measures including carbon emissions, air quality and the use of natural resources, level of innovation, application of new technology to public services, health indicators as well as people's general sense of well-being as captured in the World Happiness Index.[1] Another model of a balanced scorecard, developed in recent years, is the Social Progress Index. This builds on fifty-four established metrics in three categories — basic human need, human well-being, and foundations of opportunity.[2]

Third, to look outwards

The state senses and shapes the landscape within and beyond its borders. This involves anticipating changes to come and shaping them to the country's best advantage. It also involves partnerships — for example, the partnership needed across industry groups, educational institutions and the government, if there is to be the right vocational training and skill development to meet the changing needs of key industries. Beyond a state's borders, such partnerships may involve bilateral or multilateral agreements in order to achieve greater influence, stability and access to markets. Countries may also need to proactively deal with the impact of environmental challenges as well as migration and the international flow of labour.

Fourth, to plant for the future

Effective governments need to look after the needs of today's population. But they also need to look ahead and plan. Some common issues states encounter are: providing adequate housing for a growing population, providing educational resources to support a digital and circular economy, addressing the challenges of global warming, meeting the needs of those lagging behind amid the fast-changing pace of technological advancement, responding in a timely manner to the challenges of an ageing population, creating a forward-looking and future-proof economy, and ensuring adequate savings.

All these are areas that contribute towards the opportunities for stewardship and are crucial for the success of a country and the well-being of its population. Now, the challenge is to make these priorities and principles come to life when formulating and implementing policies in both direct and indirect ways whereby the state can influence and guide responsible wealth creation.

THE STATE AS A DIRECT INFLUENCE

As investor

Direct investment strategies and policies by the government, centrally and regionally, can uplift communities and close the performance gap among different regions. They can also help to create new markets and galvanise demand for important new solutions throughout the economy.

China's emphasis on renewable energy is a good example. It has been focusing on developing renewables as it strives to progressively reduce its reliance on coal and oil. The state is highly supportive of such an endeavour, pouring most of its funding into early-stage projects in the hope of spurring technological innovation to make renewable energy more cost-competitive.[3] As the largest solar-energy producer and a world leader in harnessing hydroelectric power, China has made investments in renewable energy which accounted for almost half the world's expenditure. Spending US$126.6 billion in 2017, China outspent second-placed US three times to one.[4] According to the National Energy Administration of China, the total investment scale of renewable energy stated in its 13th Five-Year Plan (2016–20) from both public and commercial sectors is estimated to reach 2.5 trillion yuan (US$370 billion) in value.[5] State initiatives can have a catalytic effect on environmental sustainability, as well as on innovation and business opportunities in new sectors.

As asset owner and asset manager

The state can have a direct influence in the market through its stewardship role as asset owner and asset manager. In its role as asset owner, the state needs a more nuanced and even intentionally arms-length approach. This does not mean the state is passive. As an asset owner, the state would be wise to understand its role as an engaged and responsible shareholder and not be confused with or be drawn into trying to be the business manager or even regulator simultaneously. This is a different but very important role for the state to understand and perform, especially where countries are at earlier stages of economic development.

Debate in this sphere is too often polarised between markets and the state, or distracted by disagreements about whether state-owned businesses are efficient. In reality, what matters is not so much the structures of ownership, but the understanding of its role and the quality and characteristics of the owners. Are they stewards? Do they embrace and practise stewardship? The key lies in the state behaving as a responsible shareholder, and not as a government ministry or agency that intervenes in business operations or micromanages portfolio companies. The most helpful solutions are to be found in combining the freedom of choice and competitiveness of market solutions with the stability and stewardship that can come from the state as an enlightened anchor shareholder.

A subtle challenge in discussing the state's role as owners as well as managers of business is that in different situations, these roles may operate on either side of the value chain. In view of this, we use the term "state-owned entity" to broadly refer to corporations and business organisations associated with the state. These may include sovereign wealth funds (SWFs), state pension funds, state-owned holding companies and state-owned enterprises (SOEs) that are completely or substantially owned by the government. The Santiago Principles state that SWFs are "special purpose investment funds or arrangements, owned by the general government".[6] Many SWFs are established with the aim of attaining long-term savings to guard against future liabilities, for fiscal stabilisation to cushion economic shocks or for economic development purposes.[7] While the investment strategies of SWFs may differ due to their priorities, they possess several similarities: they have huge capital and low liabilities, with long-term returns in mind. This places them as optimal long-term owners and stewards who are able to take on the volatility of the market and be patient to bear the fruits of their investments. The OECD's definition of SOEs is "any corporate entity recognised by national law as an enterprise, in which the state exercise[s] ownership, and partake[s] in purpose and activities that are of largely economic nature".[8] Within this array of diverse state-owned entities, we see the state as having roles that encompass investor, asset owner and asset manager of the country's reserves.

The state counts among the biggest investors and shareholders in the world. SOEs account for around 10 per cent of the world's GDP[9] and represent more than 20 per cent of the Fortune Global 500 companies.[10] The total assets held by sovereign investors, such as sovereign wealth funds and government pension funds, are expected to reach US$15.3 trillion by 2020.[11] There are three notable trends. Firstly, SWFs are growing quickly in number, relevance, and influence. In fact, the number of SWFs has doubled in the last decade. Secondly, their assets under management have grown significantly, by 600 per cent since 2000. Their assets are now estimated to be worth US$6 trillion. Thirdly, their assets are highly concentrated. The top ten SWFs hold 80 per cent of the total SWF assets under management.[12]

As the state increasingly becomes an influential shareholder and owner of businesses, as well as a trustee of huge assets, it is imperative that governments play a stewardship role in responsible investing, the monitoring of entrusted assets, engaging their portfolio companies and upholding good business practices. In this way, the state is fulfilling its stewardship responsibility on behalf of its ultimate shareholders, the citizens, by promoting long-term, intergenerational value creation.

SOEs are often seen as inefficient businesses. This is often attributed to soft budget constraints and the need to fulfil social and political obligations, thus, affecting their competitiveness.[13] There is a temptation for the state to play a paternalistic role in the market. This more often than not undermines the performance of SOEs when decisions are made over and above commercial considerations. This problem arises when there is no clear governance structure, and the commercial role of the state becomes increasingly blurred.

When SOEs are given the autonomy to be professionally managed like a listed commercial enterprise, they can survive and prosper.[14] With proper management and a crew of professional talent, SOEs can play to their strengths, leverage their influence, co-create value with other stakeholders in society and be a strong driver of responsible, inclusive growth in society.[15]

Two principles are crucial for the state to effectively perform its role as owner, investor, and shareholder. They are: separation of ownership and management, and a focus on commercial objectives and interest.

Separating ownership and management

Where the state owns businesses, many countries around the world practise an engaged but arm's length approach, albeit in different ways. In countries such as Norway, the law prohibits any civil servant from being a member of the board of any state-owned company.[16] The New Zealand Superannuation Fund (NZSF), a SWF in New Zealand, enforces a *double* arms' length to ensure that the government and the NZSF are clearly differentiated. The first arm of independence is apparent in the process of selecting the Guardian Board of the SWF. Candidates are selected by an independent nominating committee appointed by the government. The second arm of independence is the autonomy the Board and Management of Guardians have in deciding investment policies and strategies.[17] Hence, it is regarded as "the most independent investment authority",[18] where clear rules are being established to ensure the decision-making process is not subjected to influence from state authorities and agencies.

Authors Dag Detter and Stefan Folster aptly point out that meddling in the affairs of SOEs will likely be "ill-informed at best, opportunistic at worst". They offer their view on good practices:

> ...(T)he best way to foster good management and democracy is to consolidate public assets under a single institution, removed from government influence. This requires setting up an independent ring-fenced body at arm's length from daily political influence and enabling, transparent, commercial governance.[19]

In Asia, Temasek Holdings, Singapore's state-owned holding company, manages investments. Its functions are distinct from the state's role of policymaking and market regulation.[20] By consolidating the portfolio of commercial assets under one holding company, the government can "act in the larger interests of the overall economy" and as the sole shareholder of Temasek, with its rights and responsibilities as the asset owner. Temasek, in turn, fulfils its roles of shareholder and commercial owner of its portfolio companies.[21] The relationship between the government and Temasek is that of shareholder and investee company. This is mirrored in the relationship between Temasek as the shareholder and its range of investee companies, with various degrees of shareholding. The dividends accrued to the state (as owner) by Temasek, through its wealth creation, are shared across generations.[22] The Singapore government has articulated and consistently practised its non-interference policy relating to its shareholder role, noting that this allows Singapore to avoid the pitfalls of "political interference and rent-seeking, or unfair advantages from political protection".[23] Says the then Deputy Prime Minister Tharman Shanmugaratnam:

> On its part, the Government's approach is to ensure that people of sound character and judgement are appointed to the board, to guide Temasek's management and its strategies. We are careful not to have any role or influence in Temasek's investment decisions. That has been the right approach for Temasek, which makes commercial assessments without having to second-guess whether the Government would agree to its decisions. But it is also right for the Government, which has to avoid being put in a position where it is endorsing or vetoing a deal, or is seen to do so.[24]

Such a model has worked in the context of Singapore, partly due to its entrenched culture of good political governance, which grew out of necessity during its tumultuous early years of independence. Carefully reinforced over the generations, such a governance archetype, however, need not and may not be (easily) transplanted to other economies.[25]

Focusing on commercial objectives and interest

The state has the economic obligation to ensure that SOEs can focus on commercial pursuits and compete on a level playing field. Inefficiency in SOEs often arises when there is no clear delineation of what constitutes SOEs, as well as the roles they fulfil. Firstly, SOEs should primarily be commercially oriented, and those corporations that exist to fulfil social services should be considered as utilities or government agencies and be under the jurisdiction of a ministry or government agency, not a commercial enterprise. Secondly, SOEs should embrace competition to ensure that they operate efficiently and develop the capacity to compete commercially in a disruptive environment. The absence of competitors often means that there is less incentive to optimise performance, leading to lower output, less innovation, poor performance and unengaged employees. And while the SOEs should expect no exceptional protection or subsidies, they should likewise not be loaded with demands, goals and expectations that are outside the commercial considerations or beyond business pursuits. In a budget statement, Singapore's Ministry of Finance underscored this:

> Our philosophy is to have the GLCs (government-linked companies) operate as commercial entities. The Government does not interfere with the operations of the GLCs. The companies are supervised by their respective boards of directors, who are accountable to their shareholders, including the Government. The Government will not favour GLCs with special privileges or hidden subsidies; nor will it burden them with uneconomic national service responsibilities. The GLCs are expected to compete on a level playing field, and frequently in a global environment.[26]

Senate Properties, Finland's unincorporated state enterprise, is an example of a SOE that does not rely on government subsidies. The organisation manages all real estate of the government, including universities, offices, research, cultural and other buildings. Having a massive property portfolio totalling around US$4.8 billion and a turnover of around US$689 million, it positions itself as a "work environment partner and specialist of the Finnish government". It is also responsible for the sale and development of properties that are no longer used by the government.[27] As a successful business enterprise, it is financially independent and funds its own operations.[28] Due to economies of scale, Senate Properties is able to achieve significant savings on property-related expenses by combining and centralising facilities, culminating in higher returns for public assets.

These twin aspects of ensuring competition and focusing on commercial objectives are in line with the OECD Guidelines on Corporate Governance of State-Owned Enterprises,[29] which say that the state has the responsibility to ensure that its enterprises do not have overt competitive advantages against private enterprises, or undermine state-owned entities by asking them to undertake excessive social and ethical obligations.

States, as shareholders and owners, have the responsibility to steward underperforming SOEs. It is expensive to keep failing SOEs afloat. The costs come at the expense of the country's and citizens' wealth and the interests of other stakeholders. The story of Amtrak illustrates such costs.

Based in the United States and established by the government in 1971, the National Passenger Railroad Corporation (Amtrak) has been constantly underperforming, accumulating annual losses since it commenced service, despite relying heavily on state subsidies.[30] Its inability to build an efficient and effective enterprise has had much to do with its unsuccessful efforts to secure investment funding for long-term plans, as well as limited discretion to divest unprofitable operations.[31]

Amtrak is formally a for-profit organisation, and this leaves it caught in an awkward situation where the government is perceived as making "lavish use of the corporate form to perform public functions".[32] To resolve this predicament, there have been calls for greater involvement from the private sector, especially in terms of capital injection or giving the company more autonomy to make business decisions.[33]

In a nutshell, SOEs need to be managed professionally and seen to be operating commercially, without the burden of government interference in their business decisions, and without the imposition of non-commercial goals and obligations. The state, as a business owner, needs to separate ownership from management. It should exercise its rights and responsibilities as a shareholder and fulfil its stewardship obligations as an owner. Among other things this means going beyond mere compliance with codes to satisfy itself that the governance of the enterprise is sound.

As states play the dual role of regulator and owner, they can get muddled as a result of the conflict between protecting public interest and maximising profits. As market circumstances change and evolve, the state as asset owner would also need to adjust and manage its portfolio. To do that, and to mitigate the tensions between its role as regulator and owner, there are three possible ownership structuring strategies that the state can deploy: privatisation, whole ownership of SOEs and minority shareholding.[34] Each offers opportunities to promote long-term wealth creation.

Privatisation

Very often, the state may choose to divest its state-owned enterprises for various reasons, including to focus on governing, to avoid role duality as regulator and investor, and for portfolio adjustment. Privatisation is often recommended as a natural way to modernise an economy and take wealth creation out of the hands of the state. In undertaking privatisation, governments can strengthen the hand of individual citizens who are, in effect, small investors. Besides offering the shares for sale to individual investors on a stock exchange, there is an alternative option of creating a stewardship mutual. In this way, instead of creating hundreds of thousands of isolated individual shareholders, governments can choose to offer the same investment opportunity but with the shares held in trust for those individual shareholders by an intermediary investment institution with a clear mandate to act as a steward shareholder on their behalf. This would, in one move, create an institution that offers companies a more stable and coherent shareholding, and provide retail investors with a coherent voice to represent their interests and concerns.

Whole ownership

State-owned bodies such as SWFs and state holding companies, when carefully constituted and well-stewarded, can be efficient and effective vehicles for fostering sustainable wealth creation. These entities can embrace a long-term outlook, provided they are sufficiently isolated from short-term political interference, and have a significant and direct influence on responsible wealth creation. Due to vested long-term interests, state-owned bodies are regarded as a stabilizing influence on liquidity and financial markets.[35] They are a stable source of capital with strengths that can be leveraged to play a constructive role and contribute to long-term shareholder value.[36]

As owners with long-term purposes and horizons, state-owned entities have more manoeuvrability to exercise stewardship and not succumb to knee-jerk reactions. This enables state (steward) investors to take bold but calculated risks to invest, without having to worry about short-term volatility, to realise sustainability yields and accumulate intergenerational wealth. Coupled with a clear mandate and strong governance, these state-owned entities can fulfil a steward's role of becoming responsible trustees of public wealth and the state's overall development.

Minority shareholding

In some cases, privatisation may not be suitable or timely. This may be because the business is a natural monopoly, or is involved in the provision of some form of public good. In these cases, the government's responsibility is to monitor and ensure that these firms enforce better corporate governance standards. Having full ownership circumvents the intricacy of multi-ownership and enables the state to fulfil long-term priorities. In some circumstances, however, it will be preferable to relinquish some control of SOEs progressively. By holding minority ownership and allowing private (institutional) investors to invest in the corporation, market discipline can be introduced and agency problems that are prevalent among SOEs can be addressed.[37]

Regardless of which ownership strategy the state deploys, there are two essential challenges. The first is to remove political control by separating ownership and management. This ensures clear demarcation of responsibilities between the government and SOEs. The second, in tandem, is to ensure that public assets are professionally managed. The government has to exercise caution to ensure assets are not managed by politicians who have more than just a commercial agenda in mind.

As client and customer

The civil servants responsible for public procurement are always under scrutiny, especially when money is deemed to have been misspent or wasted. The unintended consequence is that procurement officials are unlikely to focus on a wider definition of "value-for-money". It is too easy for their political masters to be criticised and attacked for not accepting the lowest bid. Yet, at times accepting the lowest bid from external providers of services such as construction, healthcare, IT or training can mean rejecting companies which are well-stewarded and which are more likely to be dependable in delivering long-term value. It makes sense for the government and the public sector to seek out companies whose purpose, values and business model are best suited to the needs of society.

THE STATE AS AN INDIRECT INFLUENCE

Through law, regulation and taxation

Beyond the state's role in its direct business engagement, through investment and companies, its indirect role requires more subtlety. In ensuring that business activities are channelled towards longer-term value creation and away from short-term opportunism, the government has two types of leverage. One is the stewardship influence of other (non-governmental) owners and shareholders, and the boards they elect to direct the company. The other influence comes from the rules and incentives that the government creates, and the behaviours that it models and influences others to follow. The best outcomes are achieved when these two levers work in support of each other. To use a sporting analogy, it is a combination of better refereeing, better game rules and also behaviour of the players themselves. The goal is to have a market that is free, but carefully nurtured by the government, investors and business organisations and the influence of their stakeholders, such that businesses can compete in ways that create value responsibly.

Providing a just legal framework

The state creates the framework of law and regulation, and through this lays the foundation for a stable business environment. In doing so, it makes choices which can either undermine or reinforce stewardship.

It is the government which defines and provides guidance on the fiduciary duty of boards and investment institutions. For example, the encouragement of saving for retirement is a priority for government policy. Yet, until recently, misunderstood dogma about fiduciary duty has hindered governments in many countries from trying to influence the route from the individual's savings to the intermediaries who can exercise stewardship over companies.

The pension regime in Canada is a positive example. There are features of the regulatory regime, including the absence of restrictive investment and solvency regulation, that allow the Canada Pension Plan to invest for the long term, with expected holding periods of over five years for most asset classes and with a focus on infrastructure investment. In other parts of the world, including the UK, governments have intervened to clarify the fiduciary duty of pension trustees and other asset owners. This means that pension trustees now know that they will not be deemed to be in breach of their duty by expressing a preference for long-term, sustainable investments. In the market, the pendulum is beginning to swing the other way, with pension funds that ignore the risks from climate change and ESG considerations coming under attention.

In the UK, for instance, the 2006 Companies Act reinforced the duty of directors to promote the success of the company for the benefit of the members (the shareholders) while taking into account the interests of employees and other stakeholders, over the long term. In parallel, the UK's Law Commission offered new guidance to pension trustees to strengthen their ability to include ESG factors in their judgements of the risk/reward ratio in investment decisions.[38]

In the US, thirty-four states have now created the new legislative category of the Public Benefit Corporation. Companies can opt for this legal form in order to protect their commitment to a long-term mission without fear of legal challenge by short-term shareholders. It is described as, "a new legal tool to create a solid foundation for long-term mission alignment and value creation. It protects mission through capital raises and leadership changes, creates more flexibility when evaluating potential sale and liquidity options, and prepares businesses to lead a mission-driven life post-IPO".[39]

At the level of capital markets, there is a stewardship opportunity in setting regulations that cover pension schemes, insurance companies and other investment capital, in the interest of beneficiaries. Issues such as share ownership, trading, and stock exchanges are intricately tied to wealth creation and the state can play a role in ensuring that citizens have the means to participate in these activities.

At the company level, company law and regulation will cover company formation and transition. Similar opportunities for legislative and fiscal intervention arise across issues such as mergers, takeovers, and sharing of ownership, including employee share ownership. It would also encapsulate company accounting, measurement and reporting, as well as bankruptcy, administration, and liquidation of companies. The formulation of taxation and fiscal incentives should encourage the channelling of savings into sustainable and long-term wealth creation, especially if done together with the assurance that policies will operate fairly. Tax avoidance would be minimised, and the burden of tax contributions will be shared equitably.

Rewarding stewardship behaviours

Rules and regulations are necessary for the functioning of an economic system. But such a system needs to go hand in hand with policies that encourage a stewardship mindset. As Professor John Kay puts it in his review of equity markets for the UK government, "trust and confidence are the products of long-term commercial and personal relationships".[40] They are not generally formed by trading between anonymous agents attempting to make short-term gains at each other's expense. Any government which wants to go further in promoting stewardship might want to take a hard look at the changed function of stock markets, and explore ways of aligning their activity more closely to long-term wealth creation. Governments create the rules under which stock exchanges operate. Where stock exchanges become listed companies, their motivation changes. They have a vested interest in creating a greater intensity of trading activity, since that is where most of their profits come from. They gain much less from stable shareholdings. As listed companies motivated by the desire to increase the turnover of shares, some stock exchanges have deviated significantly from their original function, leaving a stewardship deficit in their wake. A government interested in long-term wealth creation could consider whether it might want to tilt the balance in favour of those parts of the capital market that are committed to promoting long-term wealth creation. It might, for example, encourage stock exchanges to become mutuals or social enterprises, or at least require them to operate under a charter in which the obligation to facilitate good stewardship takes precedence over the drive to increase share trading. Another way in which a government could rein in the casino-like aspects[41] of some stock exchanges would be to introduce tax arrangements that favour longer-term share ownership, including employee share ownership.[42]

Beyond the legal framework

There are many other ways, beyond law, regulation, and incentives, through which a government creates the climate in which businesses operate. By its actions, it can enhance the store of many of the six capitals (financial capital, manufacturing capital, human capital, social and relationship capital, intellectual capital and natural capital) which businesses draw upon. It influences human and intellectual capital through its policies for education and training, as well as for higher education and research.

The state can provide ample education and training opportunities to help people with entrepreneurial instincts to fulfil their potential in a changing world. These include encouragement of entrepreneurial instincts and the constant upgrading of skills to keep up with the times. Reskilling the labour force is an important way to safeguard the future of a state's invaluable asset — its people. It ensures that the state can continue to nurture its human capital, thus, adding exponential value to its knowledge base over time.

The workforce, according to McKinsey, will likely face "epochal transition", and by 2030, about 14 per cent of the global workforce will have to switch occupational categories. To prepare the workforce for this career tsunami, companies will need to sustain their investment in new training models and programmes by collaborating with both the public and private sectors.[43]

In Singapore, the state introduced the SkillsFuture movement and the Industry Transformation Programme to equip workers with the right skillsets and spur industries to innovate.[44] Various efforts to prepare the labour force, training the new entrants as well as re-skilling the existing workers, are carried out through collaboration among government, unions, employers and workers.

Supporting enterprise life cycles

Government policies can be dynamically designed to support companies at the different stages of their life cycle. The economist Joseph Schumpeter spoke of the "gale of creative destruction" that is a necessary feature of a healthy capitalist economy. Companies have their exits and entrances. The government needs to understand and create a healthy environment for companies throughout their life cycle — from birth, growth and decline to potential renaissance.

At the early stages of growth, governments need to be sensitive to the hurdles and transitions involved as companies mature. In a digital and knowledge-based economy, this includes brokering the relationship across the fields of education, knowledge, research, development, and innovation. Governments also need to have policies to cover the risks around the exits and potential re-entry of companies — prompt payment, bankruptcy, administration, protection of creditors, pensioners, employees, and suppliers. The state thus plays a crucial role in providing the fertile soil in which young companies may flourish. Encouraging the birth of new companies will create value and provide future employment.

The entrepreneurial impulse is the beating heart of any economy and society. Any policy for long-term wealth creation starts by encouraging entrepreneurship. The state cannot teach entrepreneurial flair and drive, but it can provide those who have these attributes with the skills and capabilities to help them fulfil their potential. It can also recognise entrepreneurs who take risks and contribute to mitigating society's major challenges, including climate change, nutrition, energy, crime prevention and care of the elderly.

The challenge for the state is to provide the freedom for innovators to innovate, while simultaneously influencing their development. How can states create environments that help promising Silicon Valley-style startups to grow, yet prevent them from derailing and becoming extractive money machines that focus only on quarterly earnings? Very often, the hand of the state is found in some of the most important entrepreneurial breakthroughs.

The story of M-Pesa, a mobile phone-based money transfer, financing, and microfinancing service, is a fascinating example. Its development was set in motion by a foreign aid grant from the UK Department for International Development which, via its grants, has helped thousands of microbusinesses to start. As a result of collaboration between Gamos, a not-for-profit knowledge transfer and capacity-building organisation, and the Vodafone Foundation, M-Pesa evolved into a way in which people could send, receive and withdraw money from their mobile devices.

Initially launched in Kenya and Tanzania, M-Pesa has grown exponentially. By 2010, it had become one of the most popular mobile phone-based financial services in the developing world.

The service has since expanded to other parts of Africa and beyond. It has given millions of "unbanked" people access to the formal financial system and the ability to create microbusinesses in areas that do not have access to conventional finance. The development of this company is an example of the second key area for wealth creation — the financing of emerging businesses. In this example, the government acted both as a steward that engages in impact investing, and as a catalyst for introducing technology that helps startups create wealth and meet latent demand in the wider community.

Having understood and created a policy framework that governs the rise and fall of enterprises, governments need to develop policies that cover the way companies are financed as they grow. These will have implications on companies' ownership structure and stewardship behaviour. In a healthy economy, the sourcing of finance, the ownership and accountability of companies and therefore, the whole value chain should be threaded through with stewardship imperatives.

The pervasive culture of short-termism across developed countries is the antithesis to stewardship. The problems of quarterly reporting, unwillingness to invest for the longer term, opportunistic takeovers and financial manipulation to raise the share price have a detrimental effect on corporate longevity.

Enron may be an extreme example, but the pressures and temptations that led to its collapse are present throughout the system of listed companies today, and wise governments will want to make sure they learn the lessons from the Enron saga. "Respect, Integrity, Communication, Excellence" — we are told these were the espoused core values of Enron. They were the words that appeared on banners in Houston. But, as a *Financial Times* report by Joshua Chaffin and Stephen Fidler showed at the time, those words do not describe the behaviour through which people in the company were rewarded or promoted.[45] Employees said that then Chairman and CEO Kenneth Lay had his sights set only on performance. The flaw was that performance, as defined by Enron, was limited to actions that boosted the company's bottom line and ultimately, its share price. A former employee commented that there were only rewards for "doing a deal that could outwardly be reported as revenue or earnings" and no rewards for "saving the company from a potential loss".[46]

Every part of the world, including Asia, has had its Enron. There are many stewardship tools which one can use to reduce the risk of similar disasters. These include insisting on a clear mandate from institutional investors which reflects the longer-term priorities of clients, changing the basis for incentives to fund managers and company managers to take away the pressure to deliver short-term earnings regardless of long-term consequences, putting an end to quarterly reporting and the attitudes that go with it, introducing integrated reporting, as well as ensuring that the board nomination process achieves independence and there is diversity in the board.

The starting point for action for many of these problems must lie with market participants themselves. However, the government has a role to play because it sets the policies for the smooth operation of capital markets and creates the options from which growing companies have to choose when they require fresh financing. There is frequently a lack of variety and imagination in the way entrepreneurs and owners are given professional advice when it comes to the next stage in the financing of their companies. The default assumption seems to be an Initial Public offering (IPO). This route is attractive to financial advisers because it offers them significant fees for the transaction. It makes much less sense for the company because the adviser's remuneration is not aligned with the company's subsequent long-term success. The other route often suggested by advisers is a trade sale of the company to a new owner. Rarely do those advisers lay out other options — for example, hybrid options where employees might take a stake in the business, or options which let a steward investor like a pension fund, insurance company or even state holding company take a significant stake and thus, become an anchor (steward) shareholder, providing greater stability and a longer-term ownership perspective.

Different options have their merits for different types of companies — family businesses, mutual ownership, social enterprise, employee ownership, state ownership and private enterprise. A government should have a clear commitment to encourage diversity of business forms and remove obstacles to those forms of ownership which better reflect and advance the spirit of stewardship.

Leadership by example

Behaviour is the most powerful form of communication. By their example, governments can set the tone for responsible wealth creation. If governments clamp down on corruption from their employees, they are in a stronger position to demand that company boards be equally rigorous. As an asset owner, the state is in a good position to directly effect stewardship by emphasising responsible long-term ownership, an intergenerational perspective, and a strategic outlook. It should strive to exercise good governance beyond fulfilling the necessary compliance procedures, thus, becoming a good example of a steward shareholder.

By exercising self-restraint and respecting the line that separates ownership from management, the state will be practising what it preaches in other parts of its portfolio when it is trying to promote good practice through governance and stewardship codes. In this way, the state can create the environment and establish policies that encourage better stewardship in the economy.

Chapter 8

Capitalism beyond the Crossroads

Human beings need a sense of purpose, and capitalism is not providing it. Yet it could. ...In a successful society, people flourish combining prosperity with a sense of belonging and esteem. Prosperity can be measured by income, and its antithesis is despairing poverty; flourishing is currently best approximated by well-being and its antithesis adds isolation and humiliation.

— *Paul Collier[1]*

Dissatisfaction with capitalism abounds. This has prompted a search for radical solutions in Europe, the US and elsewhere in the world. Festering mistrust in business and a growing perceived gap between the haves and the have-nots have helped to fuel a particular feeling that "the system" is not working for those who have missed out or are missed out. In a 2018 survey, 45 per cent of Americans under twenty-nine described themselves as being positive about capitalism while 51 per cent said they were positive about socialism. According to the pollster Gallup, this represented a twelve point decline in young adults' positive views about capitalism in just two years and a marked shift since 2010, when 68 per cent viewed it positively.[2]

Capitalism is being questioned, and its failings are now the subject of much political discussion. But the debate is confusing. It falls short for two reasons. The first is that the diagnosis of the problem is too limited. Critics talk predominantly about the needs of economic man, about financial prosperity, and not about the full range of factors that contribute to human well-being. According to The World Happiness Report published by UN, there are six key variables that have been found to support well-being: income, healthy life expectancy, social support, freedom, trust and generosity.[3]

The second shortcoming relates to the solutions that are on offer in the discussion. Political debates tend to underestimate the importance of entrepreneurs, market solutions and capitalist methods in providing a solution. The shortcomings of capitalism cannot and will not be resolved by eliminating markets or restricting consumer choice. The system of wealth creation needs to be mobilised to serve human purposes and not shackled, let alone be replaced by a more centralised, planned economy.

Consider first the weakness in the diagnosis. With a few exceptions, the diagnosis limits itself to the needs of *Homo Economicus* — economic man, whom we encountered in Chapter 1. In politics, there is a call for fairer distribution of wealth. Political critics of capitalism choose to concentrate on rights and entitlement. They attack the greed and short-termism which they associate with Wall Street. They call for an end to "casino" capitalism. They say they want to "democratise" companies and the economy, to introduce wealth taxes or inheritance taxes and tackle inequality between the rich and the poor.

Financial well-being is important. So is a sense of fairness which underlies much of the criticism. What the political critics are missing out on is the broader nature of the dissatisfaction, which extends beyond economic issues and beyond the institutions of business. People are not just dissatisfied with and mistrustful of business. The discontent goes far wider. It is about the system as a whole. As the Edelman Trust Barometer reported in 2019:

> Despite the divergence in trust between the informed public and mass population, the world is united on one front — all share an urgent desire for change. Only one in five feels that the system is working for them, with nearly half of the mass population believing that the system is failing them.[4]

The rise of populism in democracies all over the world is associated with a wider sense of powerlessness and exclusion. As Professor Michael Cox from the London School of Economics puts it:

> Populism is very much an expression in the West of a sense of powerlessness: [not only] the powerlessness of ordinary citizens when faced with massive changes going on all around them; but the powerlessness too of western leaders and politicians who really do not seem to have an answer to the many challenges facing the West right now. Many ordinary people might feel they have no control and express this by supporting populist movements and parties which promise to restore control to them.[5]

Few political leaders are heard to talk about people's need to belong, to associate, to work and play together, to support each other emotionally as well as economically. There are many problems that are not solved by a fairer distribution of income. As Tim Rogan points out:

Our way of asking the question 'What's wrong with capitalism?' has become too narrow, too focused on material inequality, insufficiently interested in some of the deeper problems of liberty and solidarity which the statistics recording disparities of wealth and income conceal.[6]

In *Ill Fares the Land*, historian Tony Judt writes:

The materialistic and selfish quality of contemporary life is not inherent in the human condition. Much of what appears 'natural' today dates from the 1980s: the obsession with wealth creation, the cult of privatisation and the private sector, the growing disparities of rich and poor. And above all, the rhetoric which accompanies these: uncritical admiration for unfettered markets, disdain for the public sector, the delusion of endless growth. We cannot go on living like this. The little crash of 2008 was a reminder that unregulated capitalism is its own worst enemy: sooner or later it must fall prey to its own excesses and turn again to the state for rescue. But if we do no more than pick up the pieces and carry on as before, we can look forward to greater upheavals in years to come. And yet we seem unable to conceive of alternatives.[7]

Judt may not use the word, but he is making the case for stewardship to be at the heart of wealth creation. This suggests a different route beyond the crossroads. It means that the places where people find employment, involvement and a sense of purpose become central. This could be a route in which wealth creation operates in ways that achieve more harmony with the mood and needs of society as a whole, in which business sees itself as being a servant of society and not a master. Here, the capitalist business system is not viewed as a monster to be tamed, but as an engine to be harnessed for human purposes. The real debate, then, is not over the desirability of capitalism per se, but what form of capitalism and at what cost, as well as what and who should drive capitalism. The questions are not about whether capitalism works, but rather how well it is working, and whether there can be a better form of capitalism that better serves society and helps address its discontent.

This leads us to consider the other weakness in the current political debate about capitalism. This weakness is about the solutions. Too many critics of capitalism call for enterprise to be restricted rather than asking how capitalism can be better mobilised to serve human needs. Society needs entrepreneurs, profit-making businesses and all the choices that markets offer. Companies play a vital role in creating wealth, and businesses as well as investors who help to steer them will be central to rectifying the problems of capitalism.

Take for example what some of the US politicians are rooting for, as they argue for a universal jobs guarantee and a "Green New Deal" to invest in the development of green energy. The feasibility and success of such proposals will depend on the dynamism, leadership and responsibility of the companies to deliver on such large-scale commitments.[8] Wealth creation, not redistribution, is the key. Companies create wealth, and if you want wealth to be created more responsibly, you will need to have a perspective about the wealth-creation process, and on the way you expect companies to operate in a market while also serving the needs of human beings now and in the future. As was highlighted in the previous chapter, there is much that can be done by the government and regulations, but the agenda still depends upon a responsible wealth-creating sector of small, medium and large companies owned, led and operated in a spirit of stewardship. In her book about the response to the challenges of climate change, Naomi Klein has recognised this point. She points to the example of power generation in Germany, where the government has created a national feed-in tariff programme with a mix of incentives designed to ensure that anyone who wants to get into renewable power generation can do so in a way that is simple, stable and profitable. As a result, roughly half of Germany's renewable power facilities are in the hands of farmers, citizen groups and almost 900 energy cooperatives.[9]

Triple Bottom Line

The weakness of the "economic man" thinking is that instead of seeing business activity as a source of abundance and a means of human flourishing, it isolates these perspectives. It separates profit-seeking business from the possibilities of creativity and all the social rewards that go into people's assessment of the quality of their working life. Both the defenders and the critics of capitalism suffer from this limitation in their thinking. They tend to ignore the positive relationship between business activity and human potential.

In a curious and unintended way, the very popular concept of the "triple bottom line" has done the same thing at the level of the company. The term was coined by John Elkington in 1994 as a framework to measure performance in corporate America.[10] The triple bottom line (TBL) consists of social equity, economic and environmental factors. In Elkington's view, it referred to "people, planet and profit".[11]

It is an influential term precisely because it gets people recognising that there is a triple context comprising economic, social and environmental factors. By shifting the focus from a single, financial bottom line, it is conceptually and rhetorically powerful. But it too can be ambiguous. It can be interpreted in two quite different ways, one with a focus on the company's productive efforts, and the other on its external impact. To understand how ambiguous the term has been, one only has to look at the description it was given in Wikipedia in January 2019:

> The concept of TBL demands that a company's responsibility lies with stakeholders rather than shareholders. In this case, 'stakeholders' refers to anyone who is influenced, either directly or indirectly, by the actions of the firm. Examples of stakeholders include employees, customers, suppliers, local residents, government agencies, and creditors. According to the stakeholder theory, the business entity should be used as a vehicle for coordinating stakeholder interests, instead of maximizing shareholder (owner) profit. A growing number of financial institutions incorporate a triple bottom line approach in their work. It is at the core of the business of banks in the Global Alliance for Banking on Values, for example.[12]

Here, in a single paragraph which purports to explain the TBL concept, we see a tangle of confused thinking. Yet, this confused — or confusingly used — concept has had influence in the real world. There is no acknowledgement in the Wikipedia article of the idea that stakeholder relationships might be important to *creating* wealth. Stakeholders are defined here solely as those who are influenced by companies. In this description, the role of a business is no longer seen as economic — the company is a 'vehicle for coordinating stakeholder interests'. This is a world from which entrepreneurs (and entrepreneurship) appear to be entirely absent!

It is reasonably straightforward when people use "triple bottom line" to describe a company's account of its total *external* impact, expressed in the three categories of economic, social and environmental impact on the outside world. The confusion starts when people introduce an enterprise focus into the middle of this societal perspective. For example, some companies claim that the "economic" part of the TBL is where they show the creation of shareholder value, while the "social" bottom line covers all the human factors relevant to the employment relationship. But this does not reflect reality. You cannot isolate the human factors which are crucial to the economic bottom line — how people are organised, trained, motivated and kept safe and healthy and given the chance to express themselves. Likewise, the human factors are crucial to the social bottom line, which is supposedly dealing with human well-being, the promotion of health, capacity building and so on. People do not have compartmentalised contact with a company through their separate economic, social and environmental selves. Companies thrive when the people who work there flourish as a group.

The same logic applies when it comes to integrated reporting by companies. It makes sense to talk about the triple context of environmental, social and economic factors which every business leader needs to consider when making decisions.[13] It makes no sense to attempt to isolate people in a "social" bottom line away from the "profit" bottom line when it is these people who are responsible for creating that profit. Indeed, employee indicators are among the best leading indicators of profitable performance.

Judge Mervyn King of South Africa, who has been responsible for a series of world-leading reports on corporate governance, is a champion of the concept of integrated reporting. In an interview, he was asked what he had in mind when calling for an integrated sustainability report, and what he meant by "integrated". He replied:

> It's not necessarily about one report. We all know about the triple bottom line. In King III, we initially dropped the words TBL in favour of the triple context, which later became just plain context. It's to get the mindset at the top of the company thinking of the business in terms of three factors — its impact on society, the financial aspects, and its impact on the environment. It's to make an informed assessment on the economic value of a company as opposed to its book value — as stakeholders need this information.[14]

It is interesting that John Elkington himself has now argued that the idea of a Triple Bottom Line needs a "product recall". Writing in the *Harvard Business Review* in 2018, he said that the original idea was to encourage businesses to manage the wider economic, social and environmental impact of their operations but that now needs rethinking, given the way that TBL has been used and abused by companies and others.

> Together with its subsequent variants, the TBL concept has been captured and diluted by accountants and reporting consultants. Thousands of TBL reports are now produced annually, though it is far from clear that the resulting data are being aggregated and analysed in ways that genuinely help decision-takers and policy-makers

to track, understand and manage the systemic effects of human activity. Fundamentally, we have a hard-wired cultural problem in business, finance and markets. Whereas CEOs, CFOs, and other corporate leaders move heaven and earth to ensure that they hit their profit targets, the same is very rarely true of their people and planet targets. Clearly, the Triple Bottom Line has failed to bury the single bottom line paradigm.[15]

Before a company adopts a TBL approach, it has to decide what this attractive-sounding term means in practice for what it is measuring and reporting under its three headings. Is it its contribution to the well-being of all its stakeholders — the society focus, or the value that the company is gaining from the relationship which it has with its customers, employees, suppliers and communities — the enterprise focus, or is it both?

We need a coherent logic to guide us through the confusion created by the rhetoric and misguided application of the triple bottom line. It is important to recognise that just as relationships overlap, so do environmental, social and economic forces. They cannot be neatly separated for any company.

As explained in Chapter 3, for any business, whether large or small, relationships are the key to lasting success. Companies need to understand and measure both the contribution to the enterprise that comes from each relationship, and the external impact that the enterprise has on its environment. This is integrated thinking. It becomes all the more important as the world moves in the direction of integrated reporting.

The real question that lies at the heart of both the debate about capitalism and the idea of the triple bottom line is simply this: given the triple context of economic, social and environmental challenges,

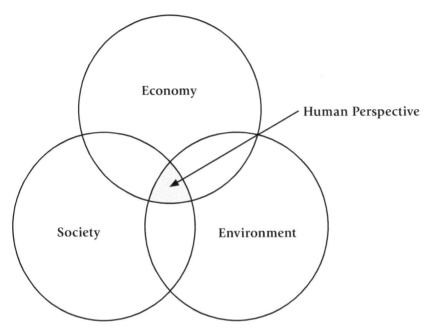

Figure 4: The Human Perspective

how can we put the needs of human beings back at the heart of business activity?

This is in line with the findings of the 2017 Edelman Trust Barometer report which reflects that on a global level, people feel that the system is not working for them:

> With the fall of trust, the majority of respondents now lack full belief that the overall system is working for them. In this climate, people's societal and economic concerns, including globalisation, the pace of innovation and eroding social values, turn into fears, spurring the rise of populist actions now playing out in several Western-style democracies. To rebuild trust and restore faith in the system, institutions must step outside

their traditional roles and work towards a new, more integrated operating model that puts people — and the addressing of their fears — at the centre of everything they do.[16]

This succinctly expresses the stewardship imperative. People do not fully understand the system and all its complexities. They just know it is not working for them and at the moment, they are unable to find the levers through which they can influence and shape it.

THE STEWARDSHIP ROUTE — BEYOND THE CROSSROADS

It is relatively easy to catalogue capitalism's failings, as we argued in the Preface. A more difficult and pertinent question is: if capitalism is at a crossroads, which route should it take in order for it to move ahead?

This is why the stewardship agenda has so much potential. Stewardship is a recipe for mobilising the whole system of wealth creation so that it better serves human purposes. Through the workings of stewardship, there is an opportunity to achieve what Edelman described as "an integrated operating model" that puts people and the addressing of their fears at the centre of everything business does. Without it, companies will continue to be born, go public and then degenerate into the inexorable and impersonal pursuit of profit in the name of shareholder value from which ordinary people cannot derive any benefit.

To illustrate the importance of stewardship, consider three problems or paradoxes facing contemporary society. The first is that we have become materially better off, and yet in many ways feel poorer. The second is that technology has enabled us to be better connected and yet we often feel more distant. The third is that we are, in theory, empowered by technology, and yet we may be feeling powerless. Each of these paradoxes is linked to the behaviour and the operation of the system of wealth creation. Each of these requires a better alignment between the operation of markets and the needs of society. Governments can create a framework of rules, but in each of the three scenarios, society will need the ingenuity of entrepreneurs and the problem-solving abilities of wealth creators, supported by investors — in other words, a better form of capitalism, with a better understanding of the triple context, permeated by the golden thread of stewardship.

Richer, yet poorer

Most individuals, if asked, would say that what is most important to them is that they and their families are well and, assuming they are fed and have a roof over their heads, have the opportunity to be healthy, to thrive and to learn and progress. They do not want to live in a world which is financially richer but leaves them poorer from a societal and environmental perspective. They do not want to be eating plastic with their fish, or living in cities with air so polluted that going out is a health hazard. Likewise, they do not wish to achieve ever-greater economic prosperity while, for instance, Australia's Great Barrier Reef is dying, or the Amazon rainforest is being cut down at a rate of 60 hectares per minute. These are examples of self-defeating riches that illustrate the problem of being richer but yet feeling poorer.

In response, the application of stewardship principles would mean creating a world of abundance in which value is not measured in financial terms alone. As it happens, the evidence presented in Chapter 3 suggests that such a stewardship focus on purpose, values, relationships, community and ownership mentality appears to pay a better dividend, even when measured by narrow financial consequences.

Here lies an opportunity for investors to step forward and exercise stewardship in order to produce better dividends for this generation of investors and a less wasteful world for the next. Investing can focus on a purpose beyond profit, and also respond to the needs of the community in this generation and the next. The stewardship opportunity starts with the definition of value that asset owners are given by their clients, which those asset owners then communicate to their asset managers.

Asset owners need to achieve financial returns now and in the future. They need to balance short- and long-term considerations. They need to determine which clients and beneficiaries fit their priorities. They also need to be aware of new opportunities to innovate in ways which they understand are important to those clients and beneficiaries. And they have to responsibly engage their investee companies. This is stewardship at work in improving the value delivered. For institutional investors, the stewardship imperative is to achieve better value in ways that are aligned with the beneficiary's definition of what that value consists of.

To stimulate progress and innovation, good stewards will insist that, through integrated reporting, they receive relevant information on the company's deployment of all six capitals — financial capital, manufacturing capital, human capital, social and relationship capital, intellectual capital and lastly, natural capital. It is in these ways that effective stewards will ensure that this generation is not pursuing or enjoying greater wealth at the expense of the next.

The next two paradoxes relate to the startling power linked to the dominant companies of our time. These are the Internet giants.

The two challenges overlap. One is the paradox of connectedness. The other is the paradox of powerlessness. Both demand and present an opportunity for a stewardship response which steers and shapes the behaviour of some of the largest and most entrepreneurial companies today.

Connected, yet distant

Let us see the example of Somchai, a talented 11-year-old Thai boy to illustrate the second paradox. He is particularly good at football. A few months ago, he stopped going to the football academy where he was honing his skills. His coach wanted to know why. The answer was *Fortnite*, a popular online multiplayer video game to which he was now addicted.

In one way, Somchai was more connected than ever before. He was connected, albeit remotely, to thousands of other people who were playing the game with him, far beyond the community he is embedded in. Despite being the member of a wider network, he was in the process of cutting himself off from his family, friends and football community.

This is the paradox of connectedness and distance. It can be witnessed in any restaurant, where a family of four can be observed "communicating" online, but not to each other at the table. Or a group of colleagues gathered for a brainstorming session, but each connected to different priorities not in the room. "Here and now" may be meaningless, as it is here but not *here*.

Throughout this book, "community" has been referred to as a core concept within stewardship. In the history of business, there are examples of stewards who exemplify this commitment to community. The conglomerate Tata is a good example that was mentioned in Chapter 3. Its third chairman, JRD Tata, said: "In a free enterprise, the community is not just another stakeholder in business but is, in fact, the very purpose for its existence."

A few years ago, Tata described its commitment to the community in this way:

> At the Tata group we are committed to improving the quality of life of the communities we serve. We do this by striving for leadership and global competitiveness in the business sectors in which we operate. Our practice of returning to society what we earn evokes trust among consumers, employees, shareholders and the community. We are committed to protecting this heritage of leadership with trust through the manner in which we conduct our business.[17]

This is expressed in the language of community as *place* and *relationships* that are *personal*. The result of the commitment to the community is *trust*. There is a spirit of *reciprocity*. Compare this with the language of community used by technology companies like Facebook. In 2017, the company used this word when revising its mission. The restated purpose read: "Give people the power to build a community and bring the world closer together." When the word "community" is used in the Internet realm, it refers not to a diverse group of people who have an identity through place, but to a group of clients or users who have an identity connected by a common interest or issue. Their membership in this narrower, virtual community may make them less, rather than more, of a part of the whole community within which they live.

The early pioneers of Facebook and other Internet giants sounded more visionary. They talked about the importance of relationships.

When Facebook was preparing for its IPO, CEO Mark Zuckerberg wrote a letter to all investors. He said:

> Facebook was not originally created to be a company. It was built to accomplish a social mission — to make the world more open and connected … Facebook aspires to build the services that give people the power to share and help them once again transform many of our core institutions and industries … There is a huge need and a huge opportunity to get everyone in the world connected, to give everyone a voice and to help transform society for the future. The scale of the technology and infrastructure that must be built is unprecedented, and we believe this is the most important problem we can focus on. We hope to strengthen how people relate to each other. Even if our mission sounds big, it starts small — with the relationship between two people. Personal relationships are the fundamental unit of our society. Relationships are how we discover new ideas, understand our world and ultimately derive long-term happiness. At Facebook, we build tools to help people connect with the people they want and share what they want and by doing this, we are extending people's capacity to build and maintain relationships.[18]

But in this "social mission" statement, Facebook is conflating two kinds of community and confusing two kinds of relationships. There is a difference in the kind of community of users that Facebook is promoting, and the kind of relationships that Tata has always described.

In *The Future of Capitalism*, economist Paul Collier describes how moral values in a society are underpinned by two things — esteem and belonging. It is these two forces in a community — the approval of others, and their acceptance and their fellowship — that ensure that our obligations to each other are protected against our selfish impulses. The difference with the communities created by social media is that people can pick and choose which community they want to belong to, and which people they can turn to in order to receive esteem and feel a sense of belonging. Family and friends may still guide the overall sense of belonging and esteem, but neighbourhood, village, street, apartment block may become a less influential conveyor of shared values and customs. New forms of connectedness could be driving out the old. Collier detects an "assault both from communities of digital echo-chambers and … a more radical withdrawal from face-to-face interaction" and warns that unless this divergence is reversed, "our societies will degenerate (and) become less generous, less trusting and less cooperative".[19]

Sir Tim Berners-Lee, inventor of the World Wide Web, has described his own creation as becoming "an engine of inequity and division".[20] The web has now evolved into the Internet. Connecting people in massive numbers can lead to results that are the very opposite of what was originally intended from increasing connectedness. The relationships facilitated by the Internet are relationships at a distance. They are not the kind of relationships that promote greater trust. It may be no coincidence that people's willingness to trust fellow human beings has sharply declined over the last generation. For the last thirty-five years, teenage Americans have been asked in a survey whether they agree with the statement "Most people can be trusted". The number of respondents answering "yes" has fallen by 40 per cent.[21]

Through the Internet, we now have very powerful companies being given freedom by the state and encouraged by their shareholders to make a great deal of money out of the creation of these digital communities. They are proud of creating them but accept little or no responsibility for the worst consequences of the design and character of these communities. In due course, governments, or supranational bodies, may decide to intervene. In the meantime, there is a role for all those involved in the stewardship value chain in tackling this challenge. It is the institutional investors and the directors that they elect to the board of companies like Facebook whom ordinary citizens ought to be able to rely on to hold a company accountable to living up to its own promises and to what others expect of them.

Powerful, yet powerless

The paradox of connectedness concerns the space that the Internet companies create, and the behaviour between users that they facilitate or permit. The paradox of powerlessness is different. This is about users being held "captive" in a larger web of the major Internet firms, with advertisers and paymasters as a key part of the revenue model. The owners of smartphones feel powerful. They have in their hand a device with computing power many times the size of that which once filled a whole floor in the 1990s. And yet, increasingly, they are powerless. In February 2019, *The Wall Street Journal* reported that:

> Millions of smartphone users confess their most intimate secrets to apps, including when they want to work on their belly fat or the price of the house they checked out last weekend. Other apps know users' body weight,

blood pressure, menstrual cycles or pregnancy status. Unbeknown to most people, in many cases, data is being shared with someone else.[22]

Sensitive personal information was reportedly sent to big Internet companies like Facebook, along with unique identification numbers which could be used to "target" them with selective advertisements. This is a relationship of transactions. Companies like Facebook have users and advertisers, and it takes users' information to feed the advertisers. In the process, the users get connected, but at what cost to privacy, and how much of it is truly voluntary in nature?

The loss of privacy and its related problems are widely acknowledged. Indeed, this has been worrying Sir Tim Berners-Lee:

> We did create all kinds of wonderful things on the web. But looking back at the past few years, we have realised that there has been a lot of dysfunction in society. People are being manipulated to vote against their own best interests. The foundations of democracy are threatened. The critical question confronting all our societies is whether the web's flaws are a temporary bug that can be fixed or a permanent feature that can, at best, be contained.

Sir Tim Berners-Lee is now involved in developing a market solution, that is, a new company that will create a platform designed to protect user privacy, by using a technological solution that taps on "a more respectful and powerful web that answers to our real human needs".[23]

The stewardship response

People have become so dependent on technology that they find it hard to curtail its use even though they know the ramifications that their information has been used beyond their knowledge or against their will. Some look to governments and regulations to deal with the problem. But what about investors, companies and entrepreneurs? Sir Tim's effort in designing a new platform demonstrates that, when creative solutions are required, we need the ingenuity of markets.

What about shareholders and boards of Internet companies? Do the shareholders of these companies wish to continue to give them permission to behave in certain ways? Do shareholders, as citizens, want privacy to be so invaded and data to be exploited? Is this what they mean by value? And where were the stewards of large Internet companies when the original decision was made to put sales growth and profitability ahead of the interests of users in this way? Moderation of the behaviour of online communities is the responsibility of the Internet companies. The exploitation of private data to enhance advertising revenue is a stewardship issue. As stewards, their boards need to exercise stewardship responsibility.

This issue is an example of a great challenge of the stewardship value chain, and it can be influenced by the application of stewardship principles throughout the chain. Citizens are shareholders. If citizens as shareholders do not like the way certain major companies behave, they have the opportunity to change things not only through the governments that they elect, not only through the decisions that they make as consumers, but through the decisions that they are able to make as savers and investors. Interestingly, they can use the tools of the Internet to do so too. For instance, the authors of *New*

Power (referred to in Chapter 3) describe how a single Indian anti-corruption protester mobilised 80,000 supporters just by inviting them to text him, and went on to eventually mobilise 35 million by inviting Indians to show their support through a campaign of missed calls.[24]

There is also the opportunity for those who lead investment institutions to step forward. The direct influence of investment by clients and beneficiaries is likely to grow. Already, there are powerful clusters of investor influence, such as the Carbon Disclosure Project, or the faith groups which moved resolutions at the 2018 Kraft Heinz AGM and stimulated that company into a belated commitment to sustainability priorities. In Singapore, the Securities Investors Association Singapore (SIAS) has, on a number of occasions, successfully mobilised and represented individual retail investors to challenge companies. The key in differentiating such mobilising actions or shareholder activism as stewardship in action lies in the purpose, sense of responsibility and the underlying values behind such motivations.

Remember Larry Fink's letter to investors (see Chapter 6) urging institutional investors to focus on the purpose of the company in which they were invested? It would be good to think that BlackRock and other institutional investors are today following his advice, for instance, in challenging the investee companies to own up to their responsibilities when there are discrepancies between the noble motivations of their stated purposes and the commercial reality of implementation. If they are truly to serve their clients and beneficiaries, they need to go beyond the usual preoccupation with short-term returns.

Likewise, on the other end of the value chain, as we have explained in Chapter 5, the boards of companies ought to focus on their purpose beyond just short-term earnings and concerns. They could start by defining what they see as the board's mandate (see Chapter 5). Whom do they think they serve? What is their purpose and what are their values? How do they balance the needs of users and advertisers? What should institutional investors expect from them? Have they got the right shareholders to match their purpose and values? How do they manage to achieve a focus on long-term stock price when there is so much pressure on short-term earnings?

In the world of stewardship in action, there will be many instances of similar dilemmas faced by investors and boards. There will be critical choices to be made by companies seizing the high ground in robotics, artificial intelligence and bio-engineering. Will they place respect for ethics and human dignity ahead of short-term profit? Or will they do whatever the law permits and leave it to the state to set ethical boundaries?

If this happens, ordinary citizens will feel that technology is out of control, deployed by large companies for profit-making, irrespective of a wider purpose. This will strengthen the existing belief of many people that the system is not working for them. Investors and boards alike have a crucial role in holding a company's feet to the fire and insisting that it spells out clearly its purpose, values and approach to the longer term, and more importantly ensure that it walks the talk.

Without the stewardship agenda described in this book, we will be left wringing our hands, anxious but ultimately helpless as these old as well as new issues overwhelm us. The critics are right. An irresponsible and short-term form of wealth creation would endanger the planet and undermine the values that have underpinned stable societies in the East and West. Without a mindful stewardship agenda and the will to act, little will change. In the absence of a stewardship spirit and its push for responsible wealth creation, the political debate about capitalism may well tilt to an extreme end of the spectrum — towards extreme forms of populism on the right, or towards more extreme forms of socialism on the left.

STEWARDSHIP IMPERATIVES FOR THE NEXT GENERATION

We need a rich harvest from businesses and investments in the years ahead. The inventiveness of entrepreneurs, dynamism of companies and adaptability of markets could be finely tuned to draw wealth creation towards the needs of our grandchildren — all these are vital to our well-being and that of the next generation.

The most effective medical treatments are those which enable the mind and body to work together to achieve health. The will is important. Just as medical interventions can create the right conditions for the patient's recovery, governments can create the right conditions for long-term and responsible wealth creation. The states and supranational bodies can set laws, regulate, adjust incentives, as well as manage expectations through their roles as owner and client. Then, it is the people and the companies they start, lead and grow, operating with an ownership mentality to anticipate needs, identify opportunities, find solutions, invent, adapt, innovate and serve customers, citizens and shareholders. People operating as clients and beneficiaries of the savings and investment process can help steer this journey in the spirit of stewardship, conscious of the opportunity and their obligation to hand over to their successors a legacy that is in a better condition than the one with which they were entrusted.

The fruits of all these stewardship-inspired steps may be described as sustainable capitalism, better capitalism, moral capitalism, conscious capitalism, inclusive capitalism and stakeholder capitalism. But, ultimately labels matter less than content and spirit. It is about responsible wealth creation and a return to the human purposes of business. Capitalism is at the crossroads and stewardship offers a thoughtful way ahead.

Good stewards will bring their ownership mentality, focus on purpose, values, relationships, community, and long-term perspectives to the table. This will galvanise companies to find ways to become more profitable while acting as a force for good. Boards, investors and business leaders can build on the three foundations that are so critical to effective stewardship — the will, the sense of past, present and future, as well as the acknowledgement of our interdependence and the part we each play in the workings of the wider systemic approach. A (re)discovery of stewardship offers the best answer to the question:

"ENTRUSTED, what are we doing about it?"

Acknowledgements

This book is motivated by experience and conviction. It is born out of research and reflection, and it has grown through consultation and consolidation. Throughout our work we have been inspired and influenced by many business leaders, thinkers and practitioners.

As co-authors, we are fully responsible for the content, and any errors. But this book would not have been possible without the examples, advice, contributions, encouragement and assistance from so many people to whom we are indebted. We cannot acknowledge everyone by name, but we would like to appreciate four groups of people.

First there are the many leaders and practitioners who have inspired us, individually and jointly in our respective stewardship journeys. We are humbled as we look back at what we have learned from steward leaders around the world. We have cited some of their opinions and experiences in the book. Amongst them, we have particularly learned from Ho Ching, S Dhanabalan, Lim Boon Heng, Teo Chee Hean, Heng Swee Keat, Han Seung-soo, Masamoto Yashiro, Jaime Augusto Zobel de Ayala, Paul Romer, Paul Polman, Li Rongrong and Sunny Verghese as well as Anthony Cleaver, Stuart Hampson, Antony Jenkins, John Kay, Mervyn King, Nick Linney, John Neill, Paul Myners, Anant Nadkarni, Norman Pickavance, Robert Swannell, Tim Wates, and Andy Wood.

We are indebted to many scholars and thinkers. We are grateful to those who permitted us to quote from personal communication, and those whose work we have researched and cited. We could not cite all the work that we have delved into, but would particularly highlight people who have stimulated our thinking — Dominic Barton, Paul Collier, John Elkington, Haruo Funabashi, David Grayson, Charles Handy, Matthew Kilgour, and Tom Levitt. Peter Ward, Didier Cossin, and Steen Thomsen have been a source of valued advice and support. Original Members of the Tomorrow's Company 2020 Stewardship Group whose work appears here include Peter Butler, Amra Balic, Frank Curtiss, Deborah Gilshan, Daniel Summerfield, Bob Monks, Anita Skipper, and Simon Wong. In the same way the chapter on *The Board as Steward* owes much to members of the Tomorrow's Company Good Governance Forum, including Peter Cheese, Richard Emerton, Bob Garratt, Philip Goldenberg Sir John Egan, Julian Henwood, Patrick Haighton, Oonagh Harpur, Bobby Reddy, and Richard Sykes. We have also tapped rich insights from those participating in the

Stewardship Principles for Family Businesses project, especially Claire Chiang, Richard Eu, Harald Link, Vikrom Kromadit, Cecile Ang, Jonathan Tahir, Mercedes Lopez, Vargas, Morio Nishikawa, and Annie Koh.

This book benefitted from the foundation and intellectual stimulation provided by the able and dedicated people from the two thought leadership centres, one based in London and the other in Singapore. Our sincere thanks to the people from Tomorrow's Company and Stewardship Asia Centre — the respective board of directors, our colleagues, our partners and friends for their committed effort in building the knowledge base and promoting stewardship ideas across frontiers. We appreciate the guidance from Stewardship Asia Centre's chairman, Hsieh Fu Hua and the current directors, Simon Israel and Chan Wai Ching. From Tomorrow's Company, we appreciate the guidance from chairs Barrie Collins, James Wates, and John Williams, as well as the professional research support of Scarlett Brown, Pat Cleverly, Laurie Fitzjohn Sykes, Arthur Probert, and Philip Sadler, and the practical help from Claire Dobson, Francesca Fitzgerald, and Beth Lance.

We would also like to express our heartfelt thanks to Joanna Soh and Yancy Toh, together with Veena Nair and Chow Jau Loong from the Stewardship Asia Research team, who devoted hours to coordination, research, and editorial work. Our thanks to Paul Lee, who has critically reviewed the drafts. We appreciate their professionalism and patience, especially when the going was tough.

The time and effort devoted to writing the book demanded much from our respective families, and we appreciate the ideas, support, tolerance and encouragement throughout the process from Conca (Mark's wife) and Ireine (Boon Hwee's wife).

Writing this book has felt like an expedition, with its moments of challenge and frustration, and also discovery. We thank all those whose contributions and inspiration have made this journey both achievable and satisfying.

Mark Goyder and **Ong Boon Hwee**

About the Authors

Ong Boon Hwee, Chief Executive Officer
Stewardship Asia Centre, Singapore

Mr Ong Boon Hwee is the CEO of Stewardship Asia Centre (SAC), a Singapore-based thought leadership centre supported by Temasek Trust. SAC focuses on promoting stewardship and governance across Asia. Dedicated to inspiring and leading change, Mr Ong directs SAC's efforts towards propagating the concept of responsible wealth creation so that organisations can create economic and societal value over time to benefit the wider community and future generations.

In his varied professional career, Mr Ong has extensive working experience in the civil service as well as the commercial sector. Prior to establishing SAC, Mr Ong was managing his own consultancy firm focusing on leadership development, organisational capacity-building, and strategic planning. He was also the COO of Singapore Power (SP) overseeing SP's business operations in Singapore as well as driving the business growth of SP Global-Solutions, which was SP's regional consultancy arm.

At Temasek Holdings, Mr Ong was the Managing Director responsible for Strategic Relations, and concurrently the CEO of Temasek Management Services which managed subsidiaries of diverse businesses including logistics, IT, training and consulting. He also contributed to the establishment of new institutions including the Business Leadership Centre and the Wealth Management Institute. In his earlier military career, Brigadier-General Ong held various key command and staff positions in the Singapore Armed Forces and Ministry of Defence.

Over the last two decades, Mr Ong has served on the boards of companies of diverse sectors including infrastructure, technology, security, telecoms and learning institutes. He also served on the boards of, and had actively contributed to non-profit organisations including research agencies, foundations, universities and youth development institutions.

Mr Ong is the co-author of the book — *Inspiring Stewardship* and has published a number of papers and articles on stewardship. He has a First-Class Honours in Economics from the National University of Singapore, and a Master's Degree in Military Arts and Science from the United States Command and General Staff College.

Mark Goyder
Founder of Tomorrow's Company

Mr Mark Goyder is the founder and trustee of Tomorrow's Company (TC), a London-based business think tank which he founded in 1996 and led until his retirement in 2017. TC works with business leaders, investors, policymakers and other partners to champion the importance of business purpose beyond profit, as well as to inspire and lead businesses to be a force for good in society.

TC has paved the way for the redefinition of directors' duties in the UK's Companies Act as well as the emergence of the UN Principles of Responsible Investment and Stewardship Code in the United Kingdom. It has organised a series of business-led inquiries, including *Restoring Trust: Investment in the twenty-first century* and *Tomorrow's Global Company: Challenges and Choices.*

Mr Goyder has also held advisory roles, acting as a critical friend when working with leaders in British Airways, British Telecommunications, Camelot, Novo Nordisk and Walgreens Boots Alliance.

Prior to establishing TC, he had spent fifteen years as a manager in manufacturing. He had an active political career serving as a Kent County Councillor and was an occasional Times of London columnist. A prolific speaker, he has addressed audiences all over the world. He was awarded the Institute of Management Studies Tillers Millennium Trophy for best speaker.

In recent years, Mr Goyder has concentrated on the issue of board and investor responsibilities for stewardship. In 2010, TC brought together a group of institutional investors to form the Stewardship Alliance. Mr Goyder later co-authored a report with the Institute for Family Business on Family Business Stewardship. He is also the author of the book — *Living Tomorrow's Company: Rediscovering the Human Purposes of Business.*

Mr Goyder has a degree in Economics and Social and Political Science from the University of Cambridge. In 2019, his work has been recognised by the award of an Honorary Doctorate in Civil Law by the University of East Anglia.

Endnotes

Preface

1 Dickens, C. (1859). *A Tale Of Two Cities*. London: Chapman and Hall.

2 Business & Sustainable Development Commission. (2017). Better Business Better World. Retrieved from http://report.businesscommission.org/uploads/BetterBiz-BetterWorld_170215_012417.pdf

3 Ibid.

Chapter 1

1 Tomorrow's Company. (n.d.) About Us. Retrieved from https://www.tomorrowscompany.com/about-us/

2 Bennedsen, M. (2016, December 20). Enduring firms transfer assets and knowledge effectively. *INSEAD Knowledge*. Retrieved from https://knowledge.insead.edu/family-business/enduring-firms-transfer-assets-and-knowledge-effectively-5097?mc_cid=c5aa4ed9f9&mc_eid=4540e4dab2

3 Hoshi, Z. (2018, October 2). Personal interview with Ong B.H., Stewardship Asia Centre. Retrieved from https://youtu.be/k221gZ_SGJo

4 O'Hara, T. (2015, June 28). Outline of Ho-shi Ryokan and its spirit of 'Omotenashi (Hospitality)'. *The Henokiens: International Association of Bicentenary Family Companies*. Retrieved from https://www.henokiens.com

5 Bastin, M. (2016, March 8). Chinese takeovers of overseas brands worthy of attention. *The Telegraph*. Retrieved from https://www.telegraph.co.uk/china-watch/business/chinese-takeovers-of-overseas-brands/

6 Paulo, D. A. (2018, October 25). How a Chinese fridge factory prevailed over General Electric, once the world's best firm. *Channel NewsAsia*. Retrieved from https://www.channelnewsasia.com

7 Haier and higher. (2013, October 11). *The Economist*. Retrieved from https://www.economist.com/business/2013/10/11/haier-and-higher

8 Haier ranked in Brandz top 100 most valuable brands. (2019, June 14). *Business Wire*. Retrieved from https://www.businesswire.com/news/home/20190612005291/en/Haier-Ranked-BrandZ-Top-100-Valuable-Brands

9 Zhou, Y. (2017). Haier's management model of Rendanheyi: From sea to iceberg. *Management and Organisation Review, 13*(3), 687–688.

10 Ibid., p. 687.

11 Corporate Knights, a Toronto-based media and investment advisory firm, gave Siemens the ninth spot in its yearly index of the "Global 100 most sustainable corporations in the world" in 2018. This index is announced annually on the sidelines of the World Economic Forum.

12 Siemens. (2018). Sustainability Information 2018. Retrieved from https://www.siemens.com/investor/pool/en/investor_relations/siemens_sustainability_information2018.pdf

13 Siemens. (n.d.). Practicing sustainability — In the interest of future generations. Retrieved from https://new.siemens.com/global/en/company/sustainability.html

14 Ayala, J. Z. (2011, September 1). Water for life. *Havard Business School*. Retrieved from https://www.alumni.hbs.edu/stories/Pages/story-bulletin.aspx?num=907

15 Cossin, D., & Ong B. H. (2016). Stewardship Principles. In *Inspiring Stewardship* (p. 52). Chichester, West Sussex: John Wiley & Sons.

16 Ayala, J. A. Z. (2017). Inspiring stewardship: The Ayala story. In Stewardship Asia Centre (Ed.). *Enduring Principles in Changing Times*. Speech presented at the Stewardship Asia Roundtable 2017 (pp. 10–11). Singapore: Qi Integrated. Retrieved from https://www.stewardshipasia.com.sg/sites/default/files/Stewardship%20Asia%20RT%202017%20Insights.pdf

17 As told by CEO Jaime Augusto Zobel de Ayala to Mr. Ong Boon Hwee.

18 Finnigan, M. (2014, October 22). Ayala Corporation wins IMD-Lombard Odier Family Business Award. *Campden FB*. Retrieved from http://www.campdenfb.com/article/ayala-corporation-wins-imd-lombard-odier-family-business-award

19 Cossin, D., & Ong B. H. (2016). Stewardship principles. In *Inspiring stewardship* (p. 48). Chichester, West Sussex: John Wiley & Sons.

20 Ibid., p. 82

21 Temasek Holdings. (n.d.). Temasek Review 2018. Retrieved from https://www.temasek.com.sg/en/news-and-views/news-room/news/2018/temasek-review-2018--record-net-portfolio-value-of-s-308-billion.html

22 Moody's Investors Service. (2018, October 16). Rating Action: Moody's assigns Aaa rating to Temasek's proposed SGD Bond offering. *Moody's*. Retrieved from https://www.moodys.com/research/Moodys-assigns-Aaa-rating-to-Temaseks-proposed-SGD-Bond-offering--PR_389476

23 Temasek Holdings. (n.d.). From Our Chairman. Retrieved from https://www.temasekreview.com.sg/overview/from-our-chairman.html

24 Stewardship Asia Centre. (2018). Rethinking disruptions, shifting perceptions. *Stewardship in a Disruptive World*. Proceedings from Stewardship Asia Roundtable 2018 (pp. 4–5). Singapore: Qi Integrated. Retrieved from https://www.stewardshipasia.com.sg/sites/default/files/SACRT%202018%20Insights%20(compressed).pdf

25 World Bank Group. (2014). *Corporate Governance of State-Owned Enterprises: A Toolkit*. Washington, DC: World Bank Publications.

26 Temasek. Our Sustainability Journey. Retrieved from https://www.temasek.com.sg/en/our-sustainability-journey.html

27 Smith, A. (2010). Introduction. In R. P. Hanley (Ed.), *The Theory of Moral Sentiments* (p. 17). New York, NY: Penguin Classics. (Original work published 1759)

28 Pressman, E. R. (Producer), & Stone, O. (Director). (1987). *Wall Street* [Motion Picture]. United States: 20th Century Fox.

29 Friedman, M. (2002). *Capitalism and freedom: Fortieth anniversary edition*. Chicago, IL: The University of Chicago Press. (Original work published 1962). Quote later exposed to a larger audience 1970 article. See, Friedman, M. (1970, September 13). The social responsibility of business is to increase its profits. *The New York Times Magazine*. Retrieved from http://umich.edu/~thecore/doc/Friedman.pdf

30 Jope and glory. (2018, November 29). Lex Column. *Financial Times*. Retrieved from https://www.ft.com/content/3166e920-f3d0-11e8-ae55-df4bf40f9d0d

Chapter 2

1   This is based on Gandhi's quote: "If we could change ourselves, the tendencies in the world would also change. As a man changes his own nature, so does the attitude of the world change towards him. ... We need not wait to see what others do." Please refer to Publication Division, Government of India (1999). General Knowledge about Health XXXII: Accidents Snake-Bite. In *The Collected Works of Mahatma Gandhi*, Volume 13, 12 March 1913 to 25 December 1913 (pp. 241). New Delhi: Publications Division, Government of India. Retrieved from https://www.gandhiashramsevagram.org/gandhi-literature/collected-works-of-mahatma-gandhi-volume-1-to-98.php.

2   Funabashi, H. (2009). *Timeless ventures: 32 Japanese companies that Imbibed 8 principles of longevity* (p. 1, 21, 35, 51, 65, 81, 101, 117). New Delhi, Delhi: Tata McGraw-Hill Publishing Company.

3   *Timeless Ventures* was first published in Japan in 2003. The English translation was published in India in 2009. A synopsis of the eight principles, on which Box 1 is based, then appeared in *Living Tomorrow's Company — Rediscovering the Human Purposes of Business* by Mark Goyder (Knowledge Partners, 2013). That synopsis was prepared in collaboration with Anant Nadkarni, then of Tata Sons, who initiated, and worked closely with the author, on the translation.

4   Funabashi, H. (2009). *Timeless ventures: 32 Japanese companies that Imbibed 8 principles of longevity* (p. 1, 21, 35, 51, 65, 81, 101, 117). New Delhi, Delhi: Tata McGraw-Hill Publishing Company.

5   Ibid.

6   Ibid.

7   Ibid.

8   Ibid.

9   Ibid.

10 Ibid.

11 Ibid.

12 Ibid.

13 Ibid.

14 Ibid.

15 Ibid.

16 Tomorrow's Company. (2018, April 23). The courage of their convictions — How purposeful companies can prosper in an

uncertain world. Retrieved from https://www.tomorrowscompany. com/publication/the-courage-of-their-convictions/

17 Stewardship Asia Centre. (2017). The 7 traits of enduring family businesses: Key factors for effective steward leadership in business. Retrieved from https://www.stewardshipasia.com.sg/sites/default/ files/Asian%20Family%20Business%20Report.pdf

18 Eu Yan Sang. About us. (n.d.) Retrieved from https://www.euyansang.com.sg/en/about-us/eyscorporate1.html

19 Yeung, W. C. (2004). *Chinese capitalism in a global era — Towards hybrid capitalism.* Abingdon, Oxfordshire: Routledge.

20 Ibid.

21 Lee, M. (2016, November 19). Privatization tonic for Eu Yan Sang. *The Straits Times.* Retrieved from https://www.straitstimes.com/ business/privatisation-tonic-for-eu-yan-sang

22 Yeung, W. C. (2004). *Chinese capitalism in a global era — Towards hybrid capitalism.* Abingdon, Oxfordshire: Routledge.

23 Eu Yan Sang. Our milestones. (2018). Retrieved from https://www. euyansang.com.sg/en/our-milestones/milestonearticle.html

24 Lee, M. (2016, November 19). Privatization tonic for Eu Yan Sang. *The Straits Times.* Retrieved from https://www.straitstimes.com/ business/privatisation-tonic-for-eu-yan-sang

25 Ibid.

26 Kay, J. (2003, May 13). Department of Trade and Industry/Forum for the Future. *JohnKay.* Retrieved from https://www.johnkay. com/2003/05/13/department-of-trade-and-industryforum-for-the-future/

27 Tomorrow's Company. (2018, April 23). The Courage of their Convictions — How Purposeful Companies can Prosper in an Uncertain World. Retrieved from https://www.tomorrowscompany. com/publication/the-courage-of-their-convictions/

28 Patagonia. (n.d.). Patagonia's Mission Statement. Retrieved from https://www.patagonia.com/company-info.html

29 Ibid.

30 Patagonia. (2011, November 25). Don't buy this jacket, Black Friday and the New York Times. *The New York Times.* Retrieved from https://www.patagonia.com/blog/2011/11/dont-buy-this-jacket-black-friday-and-the-new-york-times/

31 Patagonia. (n.d.). Patagonia's Mission Statement. Retrieved from https://www.patagonia.com/company-info.html

32 One Per Cent for the Planet. (n.d.). Why We Exist. Retrieved from https://www.onepercentfortheplanet.org/why-we-exist

33 Rauturier, S. (2017, July 6). Bluesign Standard. *Good On You.* Retrieved from https://goodonyou.eco/bluesign-standard/

34 Kim, J. (2014, November 12). Here's what it takes to make your down coat ethical this winter. *Quartz.* Retrieved from https://qz.com/289323/animal-lovers-who-say-no-to-fur-or-foie-gras-can-you-wear-a-down-coat-this-winter/

35 Wolfe, I. (2017, September 25). How ethical is Patagonia? *Good On You.* Retrieved from https://goodonyou.eco/how-ethical-is-patagonia/

36 Aileron. (2017, April 3). 5 Ways to build a culture of ownership. *Forbes.* Retrieved from https://www.forbes.com/sites/aileron/2017/04/03/5-ways-to-build-a-culture-of-ownership/#2e26c5f211eb

37 Hartung, A. (2009, July 15). Doing it right — and growing — in a recession — Tasty Catering. *AdamnHartung.* Retrieved from https://adamhartung.com/doing-it-right-and-growing-in-a-recession-tasty-catering/

38 Dahl, D. (2016, June 7). How Tasty Catering is serving up a new generation of entrepreneurs. *Forbes.* Retrieved from https://www.forbes.com/sites/darrendahl/2016/06/07/how-tasty-catering-is-serving-up-a-new-generation-of-entrepreneurs/#78b78a3b4165

39 The Great Game of Business. (n.d.) Tasty Catering. Retrieved from https://www.greatgame.com/resources/case-studies/case/tasty-catering

40 Ho, C. (2018). Performance, people and planet: Do well, do good, do right. In Stewardship Asia Centre (Ed.), *Stewardship in a Disruptive World.* Speech presented at the Stewardship Asia Roundtable 2018 (pp. 14-21). Singapore: Qi Integrated. Retrieved from https://www.stewardshipasia.com.sg/sites/default/files/SACRT%202018%20Insights%20(compressed).pdf

41 Tan, S. S. (2018). Staying ahead of the curve through agility. In Stewardship Asia Centre (Ed.), *Stewardship in a Disruptive World.* Speech presented at the Stewardship Asia Roundtable 2018 (pp. 12–13). Singapore: Qi Integrated. Retrieved from https://www.stewardshipasia.com.sg/sites/default/files/SACRT%202018%20Insights%20(compressed).pdf

42 Jao, N. (2018, January 25). Alibaba market value hits the $500 billion valuation mark. *TechNode.* Retrieved from: https://technode.com/2018/01/25/alibaba-500-million-market-cap/

43 Ma, J. (2009, December 11). *China Daily*. Retrieved from http://www. chinadaily.com.cn/m/hangzhou/e/2009-12/11/content_9164744. htm

44 Reeves, M., Zeng, M., & Venjara, A. (2015, June). The self-tuning enterprise. *Harvard Business Review*. Retrieved from https://hbr. org/2015/06/the-self-tuning-enterprise

45 Ma, J. (2016, October 13). Letter to shareholders from Executive Chairman Jack Ma. *Alibaba Group*. Retrieved from https://www. alizila.com/letter-to-shareholders-from-executive-chairman-jack-ma/

46 Reuters. (2018, January 12). US Puts Alibaba's Taobao on blacklist for counterfeit products — Again. *Fortune*. Retrieved from https:// fortune.com/2018/01/12/alibaba-taobao-blacklist-counterfeit-products/

47 Alizila Staff. (2017, February 27). Alibaba urges tougher counter-feiting laws, enforcement & penalties. *Alizila*. Retrieved from https:// www.alizila.com/alibaba-tougher-counterfeit-law/

48 Wirtz, J. (2011). The Banyan Tree: Branding the intangible. *Emerald Emerging Markets Case Studies*, *1*(1), 1–12.

49 Banyan Tree Holdings Limited. (2016). Annual Sustainability Report 2016: Building sustainability. Retrieved from http://investor. banyantree.com/PDF/Annual_Reports/2016/BTH_SR2016.pdf

50 Banyan Tree Holdings Limited. (2017). Annual Sustainability Report 2017: Sustaining our future. Retrieved from https://s3-us-west-2. amazonaws.com/ungc-production/attachments/cop_2018/462278/ original/BTH_SR2017.pdf?1522663027

51 Ibid.

Chapter 3

1 Collins, J., & Porras, J. I. (2005). Clock building. In *Built to last: Successful habits of visionary companies* (pp. 22–42). New York, NY: Random House.

2 de Geus, A. (1997). *The living company: Habits for survival in a turbulent business environment*. Brighton, MA: Harvard Business School Press.

3 Cossin, D., & Ong B. H. (2016). *Inspiring stewardship*. Chichester, West Sussex: John Wiley & Sons.

4 Collins, J., & Porras, J. I. (2005). Clock building. In *Built to last: Successful habits of visionary companies* (pp. 22–42). New York, NY: Random House.

5   Cossin, D., & Ong B. H. (2016). *Inspiring stewardship*. Chichester, West Sussex: John Wiley & Sons.

6   RSA. (2010, March 10). *Dan Pink - Drive: The surprising truth about what motivates us* [Video file]. Retrieved from https://youtu.be/_mG-hhWL_ug

7   Senge, P. M. (1990). *The fifth discipline: The art and practice of the learning organization*. New York, NY: Doubleday/Currency.

8   Kotter, J. P., & Heskett, J. L. (1992). *Corporate culture and performance*. New York, NY: The Free Press.

9   Method is now owned by SC Johnson — a very impressive US company that is controversial because it openly admits to testing on animals. For details, see SC Johnson. (2014, January 25). SC Johnson's point of view on animal testing. Retrieved from https://www.scjohnson.com

10 Method. (n.d.). Our Business. Retrieved from https://methodhome.com/beyond-the-bottle/our-business/

11 Ryan, E., Lowry, A., & Conley, L. (2011). *The Method method: Seven obsessions that helped our scrappy start-up turn an industry upside down*. London, UK: Portfolio.

12 Lamb, C. W., Hair. J. F., & McDaniel, C. (2012). *Marketing*. Boston, MA: Cengage Learning.

13 Puraskar, J. B. (2016, August). TBI Blogs: Meet the economist-turned-farmer who founded India's first rural financial institution for women. *The Better India*. Retrieved from https://www.thebetterindia.com/63836/chetna-gala-sinha-mann-deshi-mahila-bank/

14 World Economic Forum. (2018, January 22). *Chetna Sinha: Never provide poor solutions to poor people* [Video file]. Retrieved from https://youtu.be/x1CJbQvInUk

15 Gray, A. (2018, January 19). Q&A with the woman building a generation of Indian entrepreneurs. World Economic Forum. Retrieved from https://www.weforum.org/agenda/2018/01/this-bank-helps-women-in-rural-india-get-their-businesses-off-the-ground/

16 Chanda, K. (2017, November 20). Chetna Gala Sinha: The silent crusader. *Forbes India*. Retrieved from http://www.forbesindia.com/article/leadership-awards-2017/chetna-gala-sinha-the-silent-crusader/48685/1

17 Meghani, V. (2018, Janurary 15). Aavishkaar-Intellecap's Vineet Rai: The forester who turned financier. *Forbes India*. Retrieved from

http://www.forbesindia.com/article/social-impact-special-2017/aavishkaarintellecaps-vineet-rai-the-forester-who-turned-financier/49127/1

18 Ibid.

19 Carter, R. (2017, November 17). CDC backs Indian impact fund with $25 million investment. *European Development Finance Institutions*. Retrieved from https://www.edfi.eu/news/cdc-backs-indian-impact-fund-25-million-investment/

20 Meghani, V. (2018, January 15). Aavishkaar-Intellecap's Vineet Rai: The forester who turned financier. *Forbes India*. Retrieved from http://www.forbesindia.com/article/social-impact-special-2017/aavishkaarintellecaps-vineet-rai-the-forester-who-turned-financier/49127/1

21 Tomorrow's Company, Chartered Institute of Management Accountants & Integrated Reporting. (2014, October). Tomorrow's business success: Using integrated reporting to help create value and effectively tell the full story. Retrieved from https://integratedreporting.org/wp-content/uploads/2014/10/Tomorrows-Business-Success_Integrated-Reporting-L-Oct-2014.pdf

22 Atkins, D., Fitzsimmons, A., Parsons, C., & Punter, A. (2011). Roads to Ruin — A Study of Major Risk Events: Their Origins, Impacts and Implications. *Association of Insurance Managers in Industry and Commerce (AIRMIC)*. Retrieved from https://www.airmic.com/technical/library/roads-ruin-study-major-risk-events-their-origins-impact-and-implications

23 Tomorrow's Company, Chartered Institute of Management Accountants & Integrated Reporting. (2014, October). Tomorrow's business success: Using integrated reporting to help create value and effectively tell the full story. Retrieved from https://integratedreporting.org/wp-content/uploads/2014/10/Tomorrows-Business-Success_Integrated-Reporting-L-Oct-2014.pdf

24 Tan, S. S. (2018). Staying ahead of the curve through agility. In Stewardship Asia Centre (Ed.), *Stewardship in a Disruptive World*. Speech presented at the Stewardship Asia Roundtable 2018 (pp. 12 — 13). Singapore: Qi Integrated. Retrieved from https://www.stewardshipasia.com.sg/sites/default/files/SACRT%202018%20Insights%20(compressed).pdf

25 Ong B. H. (2016). Corporate stewardship — Ensuring sustainability for the future. *Entrepreneurs Digest*, 70, p.20. Retrieved from https://www.stewardshipasia.com.sg/sites/default/files/Corporate%20Stewardship%20%E2%80%93%20Ensuring%20

Sustainability%20for%20the%20Future%20(entrepreneurs-digest)%2011%20Nov%202016%20PDF%20ver.pdf

26 Antony Jenkins as quoted in Tomorrow's Company & Danone. (2018, April 23). The courage of their convictions: How purposeful companies can prosper in an uncertain world. Retrieved from https://www.tomorrowscompany.com/wp-content/uploads/2018/04/The-Courage-of-Their-Convictions.pdf

27 Tata Trusts. (n.d.). Sir Dorabji Tata Trust & Allied Trusts. Retrieved from https://www.tatatrusts.org/aboutus

28 Ratan Tata recalls sacrifice of staff on anniversary of the Taj. (2011, December 17). *The Hindu*. Retrieved from https://www.thehindu.com/news/national/ratan-tata-recalls-sacrifice-of-staff-on-anniversary-of-the-taj/article2721477.ece

29 RSA. (2010, March 10). *Dan Pink - Drive: The surprising truth about what motivates us* [Video file]. Retrieved from https://youtu.be/_mG-hhWL_ug

30 Timms, H., & Heimans, J. (2018). From sound bites to meme drops: How ideas spread. In *New power: How it's changing the 21ˢᵗ century and why you need to know* (p. 53). London, UK: Macmillan Publishers.

31 Houlder, V., Pickard, J., Lucas, L., & Jopson, B. (2012, December 6). Starbucks to pay £20m UK corporate tax. *Financial Times*. Retrieved from https://www.ft.com/content/ac97bb1e-3fa5-11e2-b0ce-00144feabdc0

32 Google's tax avoidance is called 'capitalism', says chairman Eric Schmidt. (2012, December 12). *The Telegraph*. Retrieved from https://www.telegraph.co.uk/technology/google/9739039/Googles-tax-avoidance-is-called-capitalism-says-chairman-Eric-Schmidt.html

Chapter 4

1 Barton, D., & Wiseman, M. (2015, March 31). The cost of confusing shareholder value and short-term profit. *Financial Times*. Retrieved from https://www.ft.com/content/bce20202-d703-11e4-97c3-00144feab7de

2 Crow, D. (2018, September 12). Pharma chief defends 400% drug price rise as a 'moral requirement'. *Financial Times*. Retrieved from https://www.ft.com/content/48b0ce2c-b544-11e8-bbc3-ccd7de085ffe

3 International Corporate Governance Network (ICGN). (2012). ICGN Model contract terms between asset owners and manager

(pp. 8–9). Retrieved from https://www.icgn.org/sites/default/files/ ICGN_Model-Contract-Terms_2015.pdf

4   Hart, O., & Zingales, L. (2017, October 12). Serving shareholders doesn't mean putting profit above all else. *Harvard Business Review*. Retrieved from https://hbr.org/2017/10/serving-shareholders-doesnt-mean-putting-profit-above-all-else

5   Garratt, B. (2017). *Stop the rot*: *Reframing governance for directors and politicians*. Abingdon, UK: Routledge.

6   Stout, L. (2015, April 16). Corporations don't have to maximize profits. *The New York Times*. Retrieved from https://www. nytimes.com/roomfordebate/2015/04/16/what-are-corporations-obligations-to-shareholders/corporations-dont-have-to-maximize-profits

7   In 1919, shareholders John and Horace Dodge filed a lawsuit against Henry Ford. They objected to the board's decision to divert special dividends into the investment of building the world's largest auto manufacturing facility. They faulted Henry Ford for doing social good for workers and customers, instead of making money for the shareholders. The case was ruled in the interests of the shareholders. However, Ford had the business discretion to set the price for products or expand his business. For more details, see Henderson, M. T. (2007). *Everything old is new again: Lessons from Dodge v. Ford Motor Company* (Coase-Sandor Working Paper Series in Law and Economics No. 373). Chicago, IL: Coase-Sandor Institute for Law and Economics, The University of Chicago Law School; and Dodge v. Ford Motor Co., 204 Mich. 459, 170 N.W. 668, 1919 Mich. LEXIS 720, 3 A.L.R. 413 (Mich. 1919).

8   The "eBay vs Newmark" case took place in 2010 where Craigslist, a popular online classifieds website founded by Craig Newmark in the US, was at loggerheads with eBay, one of its shareholders. eBay, which has a 28.4 per cent stake in Craigslist, had launched a rival classifieds site. Wanting to keep to its agenda of driving social good, Craigslist then took measures to block eBay's control of it. Both companies sued the other, "with eBay claiming Craigslist was unfairly diluting eBay's stake, and Craigslist saying that eBay had used the stake to start its own competing site". For more details, see Gilbert, J. C. (2010, September 21). What eBay's court fight with Craigslist reveals. *Forbes*. Retrieved from https://www.forbes. com/sites/csr/2010/09/21/what-ebays-court-fight-with-craigslist-reveals/#76fe575b2dd8

9   Dodge v. Ford Motor Co., 204 Mich. 459, 170 N.W. 668, 1919 Mich. LEXIS 720, 3 A.L.R. 413 (Mich. 1919). Retrieved from https://www.casebriefs.com/blog/law/corporations/corporations-keyed-to-klein/the-nature-of-the-corporation/dodge-v-ford-motor-co/

10   Gilbert, J. C. (2010, September 21). What eBay's court fight with Craigslist reveals. *Forbes*. Retrieved from https://www.forbes.com/sites/csr/2010/09/21/what-ebays-court-fight-with-craigslist-reveals/#76fe575b2dd8

11   Lee, P. (2018). Accountable capitalism. *Governance, 290*. Retrieved from https://www.governance.co.uk/articles/accountable-capitalism/

12   Ibid.

Chapter 5

1   Goyder, M. (2017, February 8). Lessons from Enron. *Mark Goyder*. Retrieved from http://markgoyder.com/index.php/2017/02/08/lessons-from-enron/

2   Barclays. (2006). *Corporate responsibility report 2006*. Retrieved from https://www.home.barclays/content/dam/home-barclays/documents/citizenship/Reports-Publications/corporate-responsibility-report-2006.pdf

3   Salz, A., & Collins, R., & Barclays PLC. (2013). *Salz review: An independent review of Barclays' business practices*. London, UK: Barclays PLC.

4   Funabashi, H. (2009). Principle 6: Continuous innovation (Change) and improvement. In *Timeless ventures: 32 Japanese companies that imbibed 8 principles of longevity* (pp. 83–85). New Delhi, Delhi: Tata McGraw-Hill Publishing Company.

5   Liker, J. K. (2004). The Toyota Way: Using operational excellence as a strategic weapon. In *The Toyota Way: 14 Management principles from the world's greatest manufacturer* (p. 3). New York, NY: McGraw-Hill Education.

6   Smithers, A. (2016, August 15). Demand solution won't suit a supply problem. *Financial Times*. Retrieved from https://www.ft.com/content/3a92d3f2-5ff2-11e6-b38c-7b39cbb1138a

7   The RSA. (2010, March 10). *Dan Pink - Drive: The surprising truth about what motivates us* [Video file]. Retrieved from https://youtu.be/_mG-hhWL_ug

8   Ariely, D. (2016). *Payoff: The hidden logic that shapes our motivations*. New York, NY: Simon & Schuster.

9   Lebowitz, S. (2016, November 18). An annual bonus might seem great, but it doesn't motivate you to work harder during the year. *Business Insider Singapore*. Retrieved from https://www.businessinsider.com.au/money-bonus-not-motivational-2016-11

10   Heffernan, M. (2011). Just following orders. In *Wilful blindness: Why we ignore the obvious* (p.87-89). New York, NY: Simon and Schuster.

11   Tomorrow's Company & the City Values Forum. (2016, September 20). *Governing culture: Risk & opportunity?* Retrieved from https://www.tomorrowscompany.com/publication/governing-culture/

12   Boynton, A. (2015, July 20). Unilever's Paul Polman: CEOs can't be 'slaves' to shareholders. *Forbes*. Retrieved from https://www.forbes.com/sites/andyboynton/2015/07/20/unilevers-paul-polman-ceos-cant-be-slaves-to-shareholders/#23b94e73561e

13   An accident with the ketchup: Kraft Heinz and its investors taste the food industry's woes. (2019, February 28). *The Economist*, pp. 54–55. Retrieved from https://www.economist.com/printedition/2019-03-02

14   Ibid.

15   Foroohar, R. (2019, March 3). The allure of financial tricks is fading. *Financial Times*. Retrieved from https://www.ft.com/content/a9f13afc-3c3d-11e9-b856-5404d3811663

16   Edgecliffe-Johnson, A. (2018, February 27). Unilever chief admits Kraft Heinz bid forced compromises. *Financial Times*. Retrieved from https://www.ft.com/content/ea0218ce-1be0-11e8-aaca-4574d7dabfb6

17   Ibid.

18   Langenbucher, K. (2017, January 22). Shareholder activism, institutions of corporate governance and re-reading roe. *Oxford Business Law Blog*. Retrieved from https://www.law.ox.ac.uk/business-law-blog/blog/2017/01/shareholder-activism-institutions-corporate-governance-and-re-reading

19   The Committee on the Financial Aspects of Corporate Governance. (1992, December 1). The financial aspects of corporate governance. Retrieved from http://www.ecgi.org/codes/documents/cadbury.pdf

20   Colchester, M. (2012, November 23). U.K. Eyes a Swedish Bank Model. *The Wall Street Journal*. Retrieved from https://www.wsj.com/articles/SB10001424127887324712504578135250702588588

21 Tomorrow's Company. (2013, November 25). Tomorrow's business forms. Retrieved from https://www.tomorrowscompany.com/tomorrows-business-forms/

22 Handelsbanken. (n.d.). About the bank. Retrieved from https://www.handelsbanken.co.uk/idaboutthebank_individual

23 Handelsbanken. (2012). Sustainability report 2012. Retrieved from https://www.handelsbanken.com/shb/inet/icentsv.nsf/vlookuppics/investor_relations_en_hallbarhetsred_2012_en/$file/hbh_2012_en.pdf

24 Handelsbanken. (n.d.). Responsible investment. Retrieved from https://www.handelsbanken.com/en/sustainability/responsible-investment

25 Handelsbanken. (2012). Corporate governance report extract from Handelsbanken's annual report 2012. Retrieved from https://www.handelsbanken.se/shb/inet/icentsv.nsf/vlookuppics/investor_relations_en_hb_12_highlights/$file/hb_12_en_highlights.pdf

26 Handelsbanken. (2013). Fact book 2013, Q2. Retrieved from https://www.handelsbanken.lu/shb/inet/icentsv.nsf/vlookuppics/investor_relations_en_hb_q2_13_factbook/$file/hb_q2_13_factbook.pdf

27 Gelles, D. (2018, August 25). Why Elon Musk reversed course on taking Tesla private. *The New York Times*. Retrieved from https://nytimes.com/2018/08/25/business/elon-musk-tesla-private.html

28 Tomorrow's Company. (2013, November 25). Tomorrow's business forms. Retrieved from https://www.tomorrowscompany.com/tomorrows-business-forms/

29 Mannion, L. (2017, September 13). Cordant chief: Why my £800m company is becoming a social enterprise. *Pioneer Post*. Retrieved from https://www.pioneerspost.com/news-views/20170913/cordant-chief-why-my-800m-company-becoming-social-enterprise

30 Moules, J. (2013, November 19). Richer Sounds business to be bequeathed to employees. *Financial Times*. Retrieved from https://www.ft.com/content/a2c7bbc6-5114-11e3-b499-00144feabdc0

Chapter 6

1 Dayjob. (2010). Investment Analyst CV. Retrieved from https://www.dayjob.com/downloads/CV_examples/investment_analyst_CV_template.pdf

2 Koller, T., Manyika, J., & Ramaswamy, S. (2017, August 4). The case against corporate short termism. *Mckinsey Global Institute*. Retrieved

from https://www.mckinsey.com/mgi/overview/in-the-news/the-case-against-corporate-short-termism

3   Graham, J. R., Harvey, C. R., & Rajgopal, S. (2005). The economic implications of corporate financial reporting. *Journal of Accounting and Economics, 40*(1–3), 3–73.

4   Fink, L. (2019). Larry Fink's 2019 letter to CEOs purpose & profit. *BlackRock*. Retrieved from https://www.blackrock.com/corporate/investor-relations/larry-fink-ceo-letter

5   Investor Stewardship Working Party. (2012, March). 2020 Stewardship: Improving the quality of investor stewardship. *Tomorrow's Company*. Retrieved from https://www.tomorrowscompany.com/wp-content/uploads/2016/05/2020_Stewardship.pdf

6   Ibid.

7   Principles for Responsible Investment (n.d.). What is responsible investment? Retrieved from https://www.unpri.org/pri

8   The sweet, social legacy of Cadbury chocolate. (2010, October 29). *National Public Radio*. Retrieved from https://www.npr.org/templates/story/story.php?storyId=130558647

9   Ibid.

10 Goyder, M., & Goldenberg, P. (2010, January 7). Cadbury: A testbed for stewardship. *The Wall Street Journal*. Retrieved from https://www.wsj.com/articles/SB10001424052748704130904574643993127344938

11 Stewart, R. (2018, January 12). Mondelez giant Cadbury 'returns to family roots' in £12m marketing overhaul. *The Drum*. Retrieved from https://www.thedrum.com/news/2018/01/12/mondelez-giant-cadbury-returns-family-roots-12m-marketing-overhaul

12 Platt, E. (2019, February 23). Kraft Heinz writedown hits Warren Buffett's Berkshire Hathaway results. *Financial Times*. Retrieved from https://www.ft.com/content/c530ca42-3771-11e9-b856-5404d3811663

13 Grant, J. (2012, November 27). Muddy Waters issues critical Olam report. *Financial Times*. Retrieved from https://www.ft.com/content/89709864-3874-11e2-981c-00144feabdc0

14 Tomorrow's Company. (2013, November 25). Tomorrow's business forms. Retrieved from https://www.tomorrowscompany.com/tomorrows-business-forms/

15 King, M. (n.d.). Governance is King (p. 6). *International Federation of Accountants*. Retrieved from https://www.ifac.org/system/files/downloads/1.3-king-governance-is-king-final.pdf

16 Stockton-Stannard, S. (2019, April 22). How many stocks should you own in your portfolio? *Intrinsic investing.* Retrieved from https://intrinsicinvesting.com/2019/04/22/how-many-stocks-should-you-own-in-your-portfolio/

Chapter 7

1   World Happiness Report. (2018). World happiness report 2018. Retrieved from http://worldhappiness.report/ed/2018/

2   The Social Progress Imperative. (n.d.). Global | View the Index. Retrieved from https://www.socialprogress.org

3   China is rapidly developing its clean-energy technology. (2018, March 15). *The Economist.* Retrieved from https://www.economist.com/special-report/2018/03/15/china-is-rapidly-developing-its-clean-energy-technology

4   Huang, E. (2018, April 9). For every $1 the US put into adding renewable energy last year, China put in $3. *Quartz.* Retrieved from https://qz.com/1247527/for-every-1-the-us-put-into-renewable-energy-last-year-china-put-in-3/

5   National Energy Administration. (2017, Janurary 5). 十三五"期间可再生能源总投资规模将达到2.5万亿元 [The total investment scale of renewable energy during the 13th Five-Year Plan period will reach 2.5 trillion yuan]. Retrieved from http://www.nea.gov.cn/2017-01/05/c_135956835.htm

6   IWG. (2008). Generally accepted principles and practices—Santiago Principles. Retrieved from https://www.ifswf.org/sites/default/files/santiagoprinciples_0_0.pdf

7   IFSWF. (2018). Dealing with disruption: IFSWF annual review 2017. Milan, Italy: SDA Bocconi School of Management. Retrieved from https://www.ifswf.org/sites/default/files/IFSWF_ANNUAL_REVIEW_2018.pdf

8   Organisation for Economic Co-operation and Development. (2015). *OECD guidelines on corporate governance of state-owned enterprises, 2015 edition* (p. 14). Paris: OECD Publishing.

9   Bruton, G. D., Peng, M. W., Ahlstrom, D., Stan, C., & Xu, K. (2015). State-owned enterprises around the world as hybrid organizations. *Academy of Management Perspectives, 29*(1), 92–114.

10 Kwiatkowski, G., & Augustynowicz, P. (2015). State-owned enterprises in the global economy–analysis based on Fortune Global 500 list. Proceeding of Makelearn and Technology, Innovation and Industrial Management (TIIM) Joint International

conference 2015, Bari, Italy (pp. 1739 – 1747). Retrieved from https://www.researchgate.net/publication/323733942_State-Owned_Enterprises_In_The_Global_Economy_-_Analysis_Based_On_Fortune_Global_500_List

11 PricewaterhouseCoopers. (2016). Sovereign Investors 2020: A growing force. Retrieved from https://www.pwc.com/gx/en/industries/sovereign-wealth-investment-funds/publications/sovereign-investors-2020.html

12 Kalter, E. (2016, January). *Sovereign Wealth Fund investment trends* [Oral Presentation]. Retrieved from https://sites.tufts.edu/sovereignet/files/2017/07/Kalter_SWF-Investment-Trends_1-16.pdf

13 Pargendler, M. (2012). State ownership and corporate governance. *Fordham L. Rev.*, *80*(6), 2917–2973.

14 Bruton, G. D., Peng, M. W., Ahlstrom, D., Stan, C., & Xu, K. (2015). State-owned enterprises around the world as hybrid organizations. *Academy of Management Perspectives*, *29*(1), 92–114.

15 PricewaterhouseCoopers. (2015). State-Owned Enterprises: Catalysts for public value creation? Retrieved from https://www.pwc.com/gx/en/psrc/publications/assets/pwc-state-owned-enterprise-psrc.pdf

16 Thurber, M. C., & Istad, B. T. (2010). *Norway's evolving champion: Statoil and the politics of state enterprise* (Program on Energy and Sustainable Development Working Paper, 92). Stanford, CA: Stanford University, Program on Energy and Sustainable Development.

17 New Zealand Super fund. (n.d.). Double arm's length autonomy explained. Retrieved from https://nzsuperfund.nz/documents/double-arms-length-autonomy-explained

18 Alsweilem, K., & Rietveld, M. (2017). *Sovereign Wealth Funds in resource economies: Institutional and fiscal foundations.* New York, NY: Columbia University Press.

19 Detter, D., & Fölster, S. (2015). What can public wealth do for you? In *The public wealth of nations: How management of public assets can boost or bust economic growth* (pp. 1–15). London, UK: Palgrave Macmillan.

20 Tan, T. K. Y. (2014). *Speech by President Tony Tan Keng Yam at Temasek's 40th anniversary dinner, Istana, Singapore* [Transcript]. Retrieved from https://www.temasek.com.sg/en/news-and-views/news-room/speeches/2014/speech-by-president-tony-tan-keng-yam-at-temasek-s-40th-annivers.html

21 Temasek Holdings. (n.d.). Temasek Review 2018. Retrieved from https://www.temasek.com.sg/en/news-and-views/news-room/news/2018/temasek-review-2018--record-net-portfolio-value-of-s-308-billion.html

22 Detter, D., & Fölster, S. (2015). *The public wealth of nations: How management of public assets can boost or bust economic growth.* London: Palgrave Macmillan UK.

23 Temasek and government-linked companies outperform market: Study. (2014, July 11). *Today.* Retrieved from https://www.todayonline.com/singapore/temasek-and-government-linked-companies-outperform-market-study

24 Shanmugaratnam, T. (2013). *Address by Mr Tharman Shanmugaratnam, Deputy Prime Minister and Minister for Finance, at The Temasek 39th Anniversary Dinner at Ritz Carlton Hotel* [Transcript]. Retrieved from https://www.mof.gov.sg/Newsroom/Speeches/Address-by-Mr-Tharman-Shanmugaratnam-Deputy-Prime-Minister-and-Minister-for-Finance-At-The-Temasek-39th-Anniversary-Dinner-At-Ritz-Carlton-Hotel

25 Cheng-Han, T., Puchniak, D. W., & Varottil, U. (2015). *State-owned enterprises in Singapore: Historical insights into a potential model for reform* (Working Paper 2015/003). Singapore: National University of Singapore, Faculty of Law, Working Paper Series. Retrieved from https://law.nus.edu.sg/wps/pdfs/003_2015_Dan_ChengHan_Umakanth.pdf

26 Ministry of Finance, Government of Singapore. (2002). *Budget Speech 2002.* Singapore: Ministry of Finance. Retrieved from https://www.singaporebudget.gov.sg/data/budget_2002/download/FY2002_Budget_Speech.pdf

27 Senaatti. (n.d.). About Senate Properties. Retrieved from https://www.senaatti.fi/en/about-us/

28 Organisation for Economic Co-operation and Development. (2010). State owned enterprises and the principle of competitive neutrality 2009. Retrieved from https://www.oecd.org/daf/competition/46734249.pdf

29 Organisation for Economic Co-operation and Development. (2015). *OECD guidelines on corporate governance of state-owned enterprises, 2015 edition.* Paris, France: OECD Publishing.

30 K, J. (2015, December 9). AMTRAK — When political absurdity meets government inefficiency. *Harvard Business School: Digital Initiative.* Retrieved from https://digital.hbs.edu/platform-rctom/

submission/amtrak-when-political-absurdity-meets-government-inefficiency/

31 Ibid.

32 Pargendler, M. (2012). State ownership and corporate governance. *Fordham L. Rev., 80*(6), 2917–2973.

33 Wilner, F. N. (2018, October 2). Amtrak reform: Attention must be paid. *Railway Age*. Retrieved from https://www.railwayage.com/passenger/amtrak-reform-attention-must-be-paid/

34 Pargendler, M. State ownership and corporate governance. *Fordham L. Rev., 80*(6), 2917–2973.

35 Alhashel, B. (2015). Sovereign Wealth Funds: A literature review. *Journal of Economics and Business, 78*, 1–13.

36 Fernandes, N. (2014). The impact of sovereign wealth funds on corporate value and performance. *Journal of Applied Corporate Finance, 26*(1), 76–84.

37 Musacchio, A., & Lazzarini, S. (2014). *Reinventing state capitalism: Leviathan in business, Brazil and beyond*. Cambridge, MA: Harvard University Press.

38 Goldenberg, P. (2014, October 28). Short-termism: The screw tightens: A legal opinion on the government's Kay progress report. *Responsible Investor*. Retrieved from https://www.responsible-investor.com/home/article/pg_st/

39 Benefit Corporation. (n.d.) Retrieved from https://benefitcorp.net/

40 Kay, J. (2012, July). The Kay review of UK equity markets and long-term decision making: Final report. *Gov. UK*. Retrieved from https://assets.publishing.service.gov.uk/government/uploads/system/uploads/attachment_data/file/253454/bis-12-917-kay-review-of-equity-markets-final-report.pdf

41 For example, in the UK, *Overcoming Short-termism within British Business* by Sir George Cox recommended the tapering of Capital Gains Tax on shares. The reference is as follows: Cox, G. (2013). Overcoming short-termism within British business. *Labour Policy Forum*. Retrieved from https://www.policyforum.labour.org.uk/uploads/editor/files/Overcoming_Short-termism.pdf

42 The *Promoting Long Term Wealth* report by Tomorrow's Company suggested the creation of new long-term capital trusts representing large pools of patient capital and offering tax relief to those savers favouring such long-term investments. The reference is as follows: Tomorrow's Company and All-Party Parliamentary Corporate

Governance Group. (2017, January). Promoting long term wealth. Retrieved from https://www.tomorrowscompany.com/wp-content/uploads/2017/01/Promoting-long-term-wealth.pdf

43   Manyika, J., Lund, S., Chui, M., Bughin, J., Woetzel, J., Batra, P., Ko, R., & Sanghyi, S. (2017, November). Jobs lost, jobs gained: What the future of work will mean for jobs, skills, and wages. *McKinsey & Company*. Retrieved from https://www.mckinsey.com/featured-insights/future-of-work/jobs-lost-jobs-gained-what-the-future-of-work-will-mean-for-jobs-skills-and-wages

44   Seow, J. (2016, July 23). The big shift from young to ageing workforce. *The Straits Times*. Retrieved from https://www.straitstimes.com/opinion/the-big-shift-from-young-to-ageing-workforce

45   Chaffin, J., & Fidler, S. (2002, April 9). The Enron Collapse. *Financial Times*. Retrieved from This article is no longer available online. The page number is also not available. As such, I would think we leave this as is or remove the link altogether?

46   Chaffin, J., & Fidler, S. (2002, April 8). Enron revealed to be rotten to the core. *Financial Times*. Chaffin, J., & Fidler, S. (2002, April 9). Enron revealed to be rotten to the core. *Financial Times*, p. 20.

Chapter 8

1   Collier, P. (2018). The future of capitalism: Facing the new anxieties,(p.25). London, UK: Allen Lane.

2   Newport, F. (2018, August 13). Democrats more positive about Socialism than Capitalism. *Gallup*. Retrieved from https://news.gallup.com/poll/240725/democrats-positive-socialism-capitalism.aspx

3   World Happiness Report. (2019). World Happiness Report 2019. Retrieved from http://worldhappiness.report/ed/2019

4   Edelman. (2019). 2019 Edelman Trust Barometer Global Report. Retrieved from https://www.edelman.com/sites/g/files/aatuss191/files/2019-02/2019_Edelman_Trust_Barometer_Global_Report.pdf

5   Cox, M. (2018, February 12). Understanding the global rise of Populism (LSE IDEAS Strategic Update). *Medium*. Retrieved from https://medium.com/@lseideas/understanding-the-global-rise-of-populism-27305a1c5355

6   Rogan, T. (2018, Janurary 16). Tim Rogan: What's Wrong with the critique of capitalism now (PUP Author, Interviewer). *Princeton University Press Blog*. Retrieved from https://blog.press.princeton. edu/2018/01/16/tim-rogan-whats-wrong-with-capitalism/

7   Judt, T. (2010, March 16). 'Ill Fares The Land'. *The New York Times*. Retrieved from https://www.nytimes.com/2010/03/17/books/ excerpt-ill-fares-the-land.html

8   Haltiwanger, J. (2019, Janurary 4). This is the platform that launched Alexandria Ocasio-Cortez, a 29-year-old democratic socialist, to become the youngest woman ever elected to Congress. *Business Insider*. Retrieved from https://www.businessinsider.sg/alexandria-ocasio-cortez-platform-on-the-issues-2018-6/?r=US&IR=T

9   Klein, N. (2014). *This changes everything: Capitalism vs. the climate* (pp. 130–131). New York, NY: Simon & Shuster.

10 Triple Bottom line. (2009, November 17). *The Economist*. Retrieved from https://www.economist.com/news/2009/11/17/triple-bottom-line

11 Elkington, J. (1999). *Cannibals with forks: The triple bottom line of 21st century business*. Oxford, UK: Capstone

12 Wikipedia. (2019, January 29). Triple bottom line. Retrieved from https://en.wikipedia.org/wiki/Triple_bottom_line

13 Tomorrow's Company. (2007, May 4). Tomorrow's global company: Challenges and choices. Retrieved from https://www.tomor-rowscompany.com/publication/tomorrows-global-company-challenges-and-choices/

14 King, M. (2009, October 10). SUSTAINABILITY 2009: Mervyn King speaks frankly about Sustainability Reporting (Roberts, L., Interviewer). *The Journal of the Global Accounting Alliance*. Retrieved from http://www.gaaaccounting.com/sustainability-2009-mervyn-king-speaks-frankly-about-sustainability-reporting/

15 Elkington, J. (2018, June 25). 25 years ago I coined the phrase "Triple Bottom Line." Here's why it's time to rethink it. *Harvard Business Review*. Retrieved from https://hbr.org/2018/06/25-years-ago-i-coined-the-phrase-triple-bottom-line-heres-why-im-giving-up-on-it

16 Edelman. (2017, January 21). 2017 *Edelman Trust Barometer*. Retrieved from https://www.edelman.com/research/2017-edelman-trust-barometer

17 Tata Group. (n.d.) Tata leadership with trust: Values and purpose. *Tata*. Retrieved from https://www.tata.com/about-us/tata-values-purpose

18 Zuckerberg, M. (2017, Feburary 2). Founder's letter, 2012. Retrieved from https://www.facebook.com/notes/mark-zuckerberg/founders-letter-2012/10154500412571634/

19 Collier, P. (2018). *The future of capitalism: Facing the new anxieties* (pp. 61–62). London, UK: Allen Lane.

20 Thornhill, J. (2019, March 15). Boldness in business person of the year: Sir Tim Berners-Lee. *Financial Times*. Retrieved from https://www.ft.com/content/9d3205a8-15af-11e9-a168-d45595ad076d

21 Collier, P. (2018). *The future of capitalism: Facing the new anxieties* (p. 45). London, UK: Allen Lane.

22 Schechner, S., & Secada, M. (2019, Feburary 22). You give apps sensitive personal information. Then they tell Facebook. *The Wall Street Journal*. Retrieved from https://www.wsj.com/articles/you-give-apps-sensitive-personal-information-then-they-tell-facebook-11550851636

23 Thornhill, J. (2019, March 15). Boldness in business person of the year: Sir Tim Berners-Lee. *Financial Times*. Retrieved from https://www.ft.com/content/9d3205a8-15af-11e9-a168-d45595ad076d

24 Heimans, J., & Timms, H. (2018). *New power: How power works in our hyperconnected world — and how to make it work for you* (p. 69). New York, NY: Doubleday.

Index